A Gift For

_____

Presented By

_____

_____

Wit, by itself, is of little account. It becomes of moment only when grounded on wisdom.

— MARK TWAIN

Treasury of

Wit

& Wisdom

1,450 **of the funniest, cleverest, most insightful** *things ever said*

Compiled by Jeff Bredenberg

Reader's Digest

The Reader's Digest Association, Inc.
Pleasantville, NY • Montreal

A READER'S DIGEST BOOK

Library of Congress Cataloging-in-Publication Data
Reader's digest treasury of wit & wisdom : 1,450 of the funniest,
cleverest, most insightful things ever said / compiled by Jeff
Bredenberg.
    p. cm.
Abridged ed. of: The Reader's digest treasury of modern
quotations, 1975.
Includes index.
ISBN-13: 978-0-7621-0905-0
ISBN-10: 0-7621-0905-X
I. Brendenberg, Jeff. II. Reader's digest treasury of modern
quotations.
PN6081.R43 2008
082--dc22

                                    2007037878

We are committed to both the quality of our products and the
service we provide to our customers. We value your comments, so
please feel free to contact us.
    The Reader's Digest Association, Inc.
    Adult Trade Publishing
    Reader's Digest Road
    Pleasantville, NY 10570-7000

For more Reader's Digest products and information, visit our
website:
    www.rd.com (in the United States)
    www.readersdigest.ca (in Canada)

Printed in China

1 3 5 7 9 10 8 6 4 2

Project Staff

Quote Editor Jeff Bredenberg
Editor Don Earnest
Copy Editor Marilyn Knowlton
Indexer Andrea Chesman
Designers Michele Laseau
& Elizabeth Tunnicliffe
Editor in Chief Neil Wertheimer
Creative Director Michele Laseau
Production Technology Director
Douglas A. Croll

Reader's Digest Trade Books

Associate Art Director
George McKeon

Executive Editor, Trade Publishing
Dolores York

Production Manager
Elizabeth Dinda

Director of Production
Michael Braunschweiger

Associate Publisher
Rosanne McManus

**President and Publisher,
Trade Publishing**
Harold Clarke

Contents

Words for the Heart

When you encounter a piece of art—be it a painting, a novel, a song, or just a piece of pottery—there are several ways to enjoy it. We're no experts on this subject, but four main approaches come to mind:

First is to consider the art as a reflection of the artist. The mere fact that a painting is by Pablo Picasso or a symphony is by Ludwig van Beethoven, for example, colors many people's thinking about it. What period of the artist's life did the piece come from? What effect did his state of mind, his health, or his relationships have on it? How does it fit into his fuller body of work? Particularly for fans of a particular artist, it is often hard to separate the work from the person.

Second is to consider the art as a reflection of the times in which it was created. How can one separate a Charles Dickens novel from the harsh world of nineteenth-century Britain? The works of F. Scott Fitzgerald from the Roaring Twenties? The music of Frank Sinatra or Count Basie from the giddy, swinging years of the '40s and '50s? This explains why most art museums are organized like history museums.

Third is the academic approach—to take the piece apart and study its technical mastery, its intellectual riches. There's no better example than the works of Johann Sebastian Bach. His genius was to use mathematical patterns and forms to create music. For centuries music students have studied how he constructed his fugues and cantatas. The same could be said of Shakespeare—that there is more riches to be had dissecting his sentences than sitting back and absorbing the full play. Even for casual observers, the first reaction to an amazing piece of art is often "How did he do that?"

Last there is the fourth way: just you and your emotions. Does the art stir you, make you smile, make you sad? Does it stop time for you? Does it speak to your life, your fears, pleasures, or challenges? In this approach the artist fades away, and so does all the context, history, and technique in which the piece was made. All that is left is the art itself and your own immediate responses to it.

There is validity to all four approaches to enjoying art, but for those of us who aren't students or professors, the last way is the most important. Sure, the story behind the art and the artist is intriguing and fun to learn. But those are pleasures of the mind. Great art touches your heart. It speaks uniquely to you. It influences you, makes you better.

We would be hard-pressed to call the 583 quotations in this book "art." In fact, many are quite the opposite—in the pages ahead you'll find punch lines from comedy routines, wickedly amusing insults, humorous responses to absurd questions, silly tombstone inscriptions, and plenty of off-the-cuff remarks from people one would hardly call artists. But each quote shares one thing with great art—a kernel of truth or insight that instantly speaks to both the mind and the heart.

As it turns out, it's easy to apply any of the above four approaches to art to a great quotation. You could focus on the person who said it, or the time and context in which it was said, or on the elegance and brevity of the language. We say, don't. Our goal in compiling the quotations in *The Reader's Digest Treasury of Wit & Wisdom* wasn't to create a history book, or to honor smart people, or to create an ode to the English language. Our goal, clear and simple, was to touch your heart.

Most books of quotations are pretty intellectual. They dwell extensively on the writers and history, and they provide many quotes from centuries-old philosophers that are lengthy, arduous, and filled with "thees," "thous," and "henceforths." These books often avoid citing "nonintellectuals" and instead focus on "great thinkers." There's no better example than the grandfather of all quotation books, *Bartlett's Familiar Quotations.* Filled with kings, philosophers, poets, and playwrights, it is organized chronologically by date of the person's birth; in the 2002 edition you don't get a quote from someone born in the 20th century until page 757!

This book is different. Our quest was for quotations that cut through the fogginess of life today and open our eyes wide, simply and entertainingly. Certainly there are plenty of remarks by Benjamin Franklin, Albert Einstein, President Kennedy, and modern luminaries known for their keen insight and eloquence—people you would find in any scholarly collection of great quotations. But you'll also find Hollywood starlets, great comedians, a few criminals, and many beloved celebrities, such as Groucho Marx and Fred Astaire.

We focus on what was spoken, rather than who spoke it. We searched far and wide, through every conceivable media form, to find simple quotations that spoke with wit and cleverness to the issues of our times. We then gathered them into logical groupings. The result is in your hands. You will discover that as you read the quotations, they tend to gain momentum. Each quotation magnifies the one that came before and makes you want to read the next all the more. You'll find this book highly addictive for that very reason.

There's another reason it's addictive. Even when dealing with such hard subjects as war and death, the quotations on the pages ahead mostly radiate optimism and hope. If humor books are supposed to make you laugh, then we hope *The Reader's Digest Treasury of Wit & Wisdom* will make you smile, over and over again. This is in good part reflective of who we are at Reader's Digest. For more than 80 years, we've been a compelling voice for positive values and goodness throughout the world. Not coincidentally, the Quotable Quotes page in each month's edition of *Reader's Digest* magazine speaks with similar humor and optimism.

This is a conscious choice. It is easy to find quotations that are filled with despair and criticism and anger. And we don't deny the world is filled with things to despair about, to be critical of, or to be angry at. But to make the world a better place, isn't it wiser to focus on our potential, to motivate rather than denigrate? Cynics often mistake optimism for naiveté, hopeful thinking for simplistic thinking. We say cynical thinking, like insults, rarely contributes to a better world.

A wise man once said, let your heart be your guide. Our hope is that the pages ahead will speak to your heart as much as to your mind. Yes, you might discover some interesting people and learn some interesting things as you read on. In fact, we decided to provide special presentations on 18 people who speak particularly eloquently to these modern times. But if we did our job right, your sense of humor and rightness will be as engaged by this book as your brain will be. That would make us very pleased—and the world a better place.

Neil Wertheimer

EDITOR IN CHIEF
READER'S DIGEST BOOKS

The Path through **Life**

Babies don't speak. Neither do the dearly departed. But many
of those laboring to make sense of life in between those two
mileposts have a lot of wisdom—and a little foolishness, too—
to share about the path through life.

11

Childhood

The trouble with children is that they're not returnable.

— *Quentin Crisp*

A child of five would understand this. Send someone to fetch a child of five.

— *Groucho Marx*

Every time a child says "I don't believe in fairies" there is a little fairy somewhere that falls down dead.

—*James M. Barrie*

There are three terrible ages of childhood—1 to 10, 10 to 20, and 20 to 30.

— *Cleveland Amory*

I have the heart of a child. I keep it in a jar on my shelf.

— *Robert Bloch*

Youth is that period when a young boy knows everything but how to make a living.

— *Carey Williams*

If you want to see what children can do, you must stop giving them things.

— *Norman Douglas*

Youth would be an ideal state if it came a little later in life.

— *Herbert Henry Asquith*

The deepest definition of youth is life as yet untouched by tragedy.

— *Alfred North Whitehead*

The surest way to corrupt a youth is to instruct him to hold in higher esteem those who think alike than those who think differently.

— *Friedrich Nietzsche*

Children need love, especially when they do not deserve it.
— *Harold S. Hulbert*

Children are not things to be molded, but are people to be unfolded.
— *Jess Lair*

We cannot always build the future for our youth, but we can build our youth for the future.
— *Franklin D. Roosevelt*

Every child is an artist. The problem is how to remain an artist once he grows up.
— *Pablo Picasso*

Any system named Dewey was all right with us. We looked forward to hearing about the Huey and Louie decimal systems too.
— *Chris Van Allsburg*

Many ideas grow better when transplanted into another mind than in the one where they sprung up.
— *Oliver Wendell Holmes*

Kids are great. That's one of the best things about our business, all the kids you get to meet. It's a shame they have to grow up to be regular people and come to the games and call you names.
— *Charles Barkley*

In case you're worried about what's going to become of the younger generation, it's going to grow up and start worrying about the younger generation.
— *Roger Allen*

A happy childhood has spoiled many a promising life.
— *Robertson Davies*

Home computers are being called upon to perform many new functions, including the consumption of homework formerly eaten by the dog.
— *Doug Larson*

It's important for survival that children have their own experiences, the kind they learn from. The kind their parents

arrange for them are not as useful. Good parents are the
hardest to get rid of.   — *Garrison Keillor*

Your children need your presence more than your presents.
                                                              —*Jesse Jackson*

One of the most obvious facts about grownups to a child is
that they have forgotten what it is like to be a child.
                                                              — *Randall Jarrell*

You know that children are growing up when they start
asking questions that have answers.   —*John J. Plomp*

I've never understood why people consider youth a time
of freedom and joy. It's probably because they have forgotten
their own.   — *Margaret Atwood*

Level with your child by being honest.
Nobody spots a phony quicker than a child.

— MARY MᴬᶜCRACKEN

Beware of him who hates the laugh of a child.
                                                              — *Henry Ward Beecher*

If you want children to keep their feet on the ground, put some
responsibility on their shoulders.   — *Abigail Van Buren*

You should never do anything wicked and lay it on your
brother, when it is just as convenient to lay it on some
other boy.   — *Mark Twain*

Never help a child with a task at which he feels he can
succeed.   — *Maria Montessori*

The young are generally full of revolt, and are often pretty
revolting about it.   — *Mignon McLaughlin*

It goes without saying that you should never have more children than you have car windows — *Erma Bombeck*

I'm gonna put a curse on you and all your kids will be born completely naked. —*Jimi Hendrix*

$\mathcal{E}$ducation

Education is not the filling of a pail, but the lighting of a fire. — *William Butler Yeats*

If you think education is expensive—try ignorance. — *Derek Bok*

Most of what you learn in the first four years of elementary school will be valid all your life. Most of what you learn in four years of college won't be. This is another reason some people contend grade school teachers should be paid more than university professors. — *L. M. Boyd*

What we become depends on what we read after all of the professors have finished with us. The greatest university of all is a collection of books. — *Thomas Carlyle*

Our progress as a nation can be no swifter than our progress in education. Our requirements for world leadership, our hopes for economic growth, and the demands of citizenship itself in an era such as this all require the maximum development of every young American's capacity. The human mind is our fundamental resource. —*John F. Kennedy*

The fool wonders, the wise man asks.

— *Benjamin Disraeli*

Education is like a double-edged sword. It may be turned to dangerous uses if it is not properly handled.

— *Wu Ting-Fang*

Some people drink from the fountain of knowledge, others just gargle.

— *Robert Anthony*

It is a miracle that curiosity survives formal education.

— *Albert Einstein*

The cure for boredom is curiosity. There is no cure for curiosity.

— *Dorothy Parker*

No other job in the world could possibly dispossess one so completely as this job of teaching. You could stand all day in a laundry, for instance, still in possession of your mind. But this teaching utterly obliterates you. It cuts right into your being: essentially, it takes over your spirit. It drags it out from where it would hide.

— *Sylvia Ashton-Warner*

Human history becomes more and more a race between education and catastrophe.

— *H. G. Wells*

Nothing in education is so astonishing as the amount of ignorance it accumulates in the form of inert facts.

— *Henry B. Adams*

It is possible to store the mind with a million facts and still be entirely uneducated.

— *Alec Bourne*

Highly educated bores are by far the worst; they know so much, in such fiendish detail, to be boring about.

— *Louis Kronenberger*

Good teaching is one-fourth preparation and three-fourths theater.
— *Gail Godwin*

Let the teachers teach English and I will teach baseball. There is a lot of people in the United States who say "isn't," and they ain't eating.
— *Dizzy Dean*

The immature mind hops from one thing to another; the mature mind seeks to follow through.
— *Harry A. Overstreet*

Men are born ignorant, not stupid. They are made stupid by education.
— *Bertrand Russell*

Education is when you read the fine print. Experience is what you get if you don't.
— *Pete Seeger*

Education is the period during which you are being instructed by somebody you do not know, about something you do not want to know.
— *G. K. Chesterton*

Those people who think they know everything are a great annoyance to those of us who do.
— *Isaac Asimov*

The trouble with learning from experience is that you never graduate.
— *Doug Larson*

The average Ph.D. thesis is nothing but a transference of bones from one graveyard to another.
— *J. Frank Dobie*

What sculpture is to a block of marble, education is to the soul.
— *Joseph Addison*

You can never learn less, you can only learn more.
— *R. Buckminster Fuller*

Education is what remains after one has forgotten everything he learned in school.
— *Albert Einstein*

If little else, the brain is an educational toy.

— *Tom Robbins*

A college degree is not a sign that one is a finished product but an indication a person is prepared for life.

— *Edward A. Malloy*

Growth demands a temporary surrender of security.

— *Gail Sheehy*

Growth is an erratic forward movement: two steps forward, one step back. Remember that and be very gentle with yourself.

— *Julia Cameron*

Everybody wants to be somebody; nobody wants to grow.

— *Johann von Goethe*

All growth is a leap in the dark, a spontaneous unpremeditated act without the benefit of experience.

— *Henry Miller*

Learning is not compulsory...neither is survival.

— *W. Edwards Deming*

Education is not preparation for life; education is life itself.

— *John Dewey*

Experience is a good teacher, but she sends in terrific bills.

— *Minna Antrim*

Everywhere I go, I'm asked if I think the universities stifle writers. My opinion is that they don't stifle enough of them. There's many a best seller that could have been prevented by a good teacher.

— *Flannery O'Connor*

A sense of curiosity is nature's original school of education.

— *Smiley Blanton*

Education's purpose is to replace an empty mind with an open one. — *Malcolm Forbes*

A teacher affects eternity; he can never tell where his influence stops. — *Henry Adams*

The illiterate of the 21st century will not be those who cannot read and write, but those who cannot learn, unlearn, and relearn. — *Alvin Toffler*

Just think of the tragedy of teaching children not to doubt. — *Clarence Darrow*

The freethinking of one age is the common sense of the next. — *Matthew Arnold*

Skepticism: the mark and even the pose of the educated mind. — *John Dewey*

A lot of fellows nowadays have a B.A., M.D., or Ph.D. Unfortunately, they don't have a J.O.B.

— FATS DOMINO

It is the mark of an educated mind to be able to entertain a thought without accepting it. — *Aristotle*

The fireworks begin today. Each diploma is a lighted match. Each one of you is a fuse. — *Ed Koch*

We now accept the fact that learning is a lifelong process of keeping abreast of change. And the most pressing task is to teach people how to learn. — *Peter F. Drucker*

Sex education may be a good idea in the schools, but I don't believe the kids should be given homework. — *Bill Cosby*

America believes in education: The average professor earns more money in a year than a professional athlete earns in a whole week.

— *Evan Esar*

Give a man a fish
and you feed him for a day.
Teach him how to fish
and you feed him for a lifetime.

— *Lao-tzu*

It is necessary for us to learn from others' mistakes. You will not live long enough to make them all yourself.

— *Hyman G. Rickover*

The wisest mind has something yet to learn.

— *George Santayana*

Education: that which reveals to the wise, and conceals from the stupid, the vast limits of their knowledge.

— *Mark Twain*

The highest result of education is tolerance.

— *Helen Keller*

Colleges hate geniuses, just as convents hate saints.

— *Ralph Waldo Emerson*

It is the province of knowledge to speak and it is the privilege of wisdom to listen.   — *Oliver Wendell Holmes*

To the uneducated, an A is just three sticks.

— *A. A. Milne*

College ain't so much where you been as how you talk when you get back.   — *Ossie Davis*

What is important is to keep learning, to enjoy challenge, and to tolerate ambiguity. In the end there are no certain answers.

— *Martina Horner*

I was born not knowing and have had only a little time to change that here and there. — *Richard P. Feynman*

Some people talk in their sleep. Lecturers talk while other people sleep. — *Albert Camus*

I have tried to know absolutely nothing about a great many things, and I have succeeded fairly well. — *Robert Benchley*

Whatever career you may choose for yourself—doctor, lawyer, teacher—let me propose an avocation to be pursued along with it. Become a dedicated fighter for civil rights. Make it a central part of your life. It will make you a better doctor, a better lawyer, a better teacher. It will enrich your spirit as nothing else possibly can. It will give you that rare sense of nobility that can only spring from love and selflessly helping your fellow man. Make a career of humanity. Commit yourself to the noble struggle for human rights. You will make a greater person of yourself, a greater nation of your country, and a finer world to live in.

— *Martin Luther King, Jr.*

Adulthood

All appears to change when we change.

— *Henri-Frédéric Amiel*

I'm 30 years old, but I read at the 34-year-old level.

— *Dana Carvey*

The really frightening thing about middle age is that you know you'll grow out of it. — *Doris Day*

He not busy being born is busy dying.

— *Bob Dylan*

The reward for conformity was that everyone liked you except yourself. — *Rita Mae Brown*

I'm just a person trapped inside a woman's body.

— *Elayne Boosler*

Being in the army is like being in the Boy Scouts, except that the Boy Scouts have adult supervision. — *Blake Clark*

Boys will be boys, and so will a lot of middle-aged men.

— *Kin Hubbard*

Don't accept rides from strange men, and remember that all men are strange. — *Robin Morgan*

The male is a domestic animal which, if treated with firm-ness, can be trained to do most things. — *Jilly Cooper*

Men who never get carried away should be.

— *Malcolm Forbes*

Men are like a deck of cards. You'll find the occasional king, but most are jacks. — *Laura Swenson*

A man's brain has a more difficult time shifting from thinking to feeling than a woman's brain does. — *Barbara De Angelis*

Life's a tough proposition, and the first hundred years are the hardest. — *Wilson Mizner*

Better be wise by the misfortunes of others than by your own.

— *Aesop*

Middle age is when your broad mind and narrow waist begin to change places.   — E. Joseph Crossman

After 30, a body has a mind of its own.

— Bette Midler

It's the friends you can call up at four a.m. that matter.

— Marlene Dietrich

Health consists of having the same diseases as one's neighbors.

— Quentin Crisp

Call it a clan, call it a network, call it a tribe, call it a family. Whatever you call it, whoever you are, you need one.

— Jane Howard

Even as the cell is the unit of the organic body, so the family is the unit of society.   — Ruth Nanda Anshen

Every man's life is a fairy tale written by God's fingers.

— Hans Christian Andersen

When you dance, your purpose is not to get to a certain place on the floor. It's to enjoy each step along the way.

— Wayne Dyer

You grow up the day you have the first real laugh at yourself.

— Ethel Barrymore

The creative adult is the child who has survived.

— Ursula K. Le Guin

When you grow up your mother says, "Wear rubbers or you'll catch cold." When you become an adult you discover that you have the right not to wear rubbers and to see if you catch cold or not. It's something like that.

— Diane Arbus

If the world were a logical place, men would ride sidesaddle.

— Rita Mae Brown

True maturity is only reached when a man realizes he has become a father figure to his girlfriends' boyfriends—and he accepts it.

— Larry McMurtry

A good home must be made, not bought.

—Joyce Maynard

Middle age is that perplexing time of life when we hear two voices calling us, one saying, "Why not?" and the other, "Why bother?"

— Sydney J. Harris

Everything has been figured out, except how to live.

—Jean-Paul Sartre

When childhood dies, its corpses are called adults.

— Brian Aldiss

If you ever start feeling like you have the goofiest, craziest, most dysfunctional family in the world, all you have to do is go to a state fair. Because five minutes at the fair, you'll be going, "You know, we're all right. We are dang near royalty."

— JEFF FOXWORTHY

The willingness to accept responsibility for one's own life is the source from which self-respect springs.   *—Joan Didion*

Women now have choices. They can be married, not married, have a job, not have a job, be married with children, unmarried with children. Men have the same choice we've always had: work or prison.   *— Tim Allen*

If you surveyed a hundred typical middle-aged Americans, I bet you'd find that only two of them could tell you their blood types, but every last one of them would know the theme song from *The Beverly Hillbillies*.   — *Dave Barry*

Middle age occurs when you are too young to take up golf and too old to rush up to the net.   — *Franklin P. Adams*

Habits are safer than rules; you don't have to watch them. And you don't have to keep them either. They keep you.
           — *Frank Crane*

The future is like heaven—everyone exalts it, but no one wants to go there now.   — *James A. Baldwin*

Life is what happens to you while you're busy making other plans.   — *John Lennon*

It's too bad I'm not as wonderful a person as people say I am, because the world could use a few people like that.
           — *Alan Alda*

Every generation imagines itself to be more intelligent than the one that went before it, and wiser than the one that comes after it.   — *George Orwell*

Middle age is when you've met so many people that every new person you meet reminds you of someone else.
           — *Ogden Nash*

A safe but sometimes chilly way of recalling the past is to force open a crammed drawer. If you are searching for anything in particular you don't find it, but something falls out at the back that is often more interesting.
           — *James M. Barrie*

Philosophers are adults who persist in asking childish questions.   — *Isaiah Berlin*

The youth of the present day are quite monstrous. They have absolutely no respect for dyed hair. — *Oscar Wilde*

Back in the 1960s, birthday parties were major fun. The Grateful Dead was on the hi-fi and you danced and took powerful drugs and swam naked in the lake and lay on the sand talking about what you were feeling. But I can't do that anymore for fear of embarrassing my children.
— *Garrison Keillor*

The man who views the world at 50 the same as he did at 20 has wasted 30 years of his life. — *Muhammad Ali*

Maturity begins to grow when you can sense your concern for others outweighing your concern for yourself.
— *John MacNaughton*

Imagination grows by exercise and, contrary to common belief, is more powerful in the mature than in the young.
— *W. Somerset Maugham*

Acting is a masochistic form of exhibitionism. It is not quite the occupation of an adult. — *Laurence Olivier*

*L*ove

The only time a woman really succeeds in changing a man is when he's a baby. — *Natalie Wood*

Most women set out to try to change a man, and when they have changed him they do not like him. — *Marlene Dietrich*

The only thing worse than a man you can't control is a man you can. — *Margo Kaufman*

Love is an irresistible desire to be irresistibly desired. — *Robert Frost*

We are most alive when we're in love. — *John Updike*

Love is an act of endless forgiveness, a tender look which becomes a habit. — *Peter Ustinov*

I love Mickey Mouse more than any woman I have ever known. — *Walt Disney*

If you aren't good at loving yourself, you will have a difficult time loving anyone, since you'll resent the time and energy you give another person that you aren't even giving to yourself. — *Barbara De Angelis*

You will find as you look back upon your life that the moments when you have truly lived are the moments when you have done things in the spirit of love. — *Henry Drummond*

Love is staying up all night with a sick child—or a healthy adult. — *David Frost*

When you love a man, he becomes more than a body. His physical limbs expand, and his outline recedes, vanishes. He is rich and sweet and right. He is part of the world, the atmosphere, the blue sky and the blue water. — *Gwendolyn Brooks*

Love does not begin and end the way we seem to think it does. Love is a battle, love is a war; love is a growing up.

— *James Baldwin*

There is a rule in sailing where the more maneuverable ship should give way to the less maneuverable craft. I think this is sometimes a good rule to follow in human relationships as well.

— *Joyce Brothers*

Nobody will ever win the battle of the sexes. There's too much fraternizing with the enemy.

— *Henry Kissinger*

Love him and let him love you. Do you think anything else under heaven really matters?

— *James Baldwin*

Among those whom I like or admire, I can find no common denominator, but among those whom I love, I can: All of them make me laugh.

— *W. H. Auden*

Love means not ever having to say you're sorry.

— *Erich Segal*

The first duty of love is to listen.

— *Paul Tillich*

The moment we choose to love we begin to move towards freedom.

— *Bell Hooks*

Sex is a momentary itch; love never lets you go.

— *Kingsley Amis*

If grass can grow through cement, love can find you at every time in your life.

— *Cher*

Friendship is certainly the finest balm for the pangs of disappointed love.

— *Jane Austen*

Looking back, I have this to regret, that too often when I loved, I did not say so. — *David Grayson*

It is probably not love that makes the world go around, but rather those mutually supportive alliances through which partners recognize their dependence on each other for the achievement of shared and private goals. — *Fred Allen*

Love doesn't just sit there, like a stone; it has to be made, like bread, remade all the time, made new. — *Ursula K. Le Guin*

To love is to receive a glimpse of heaven.
— *Karen Sunde*

To love and be loved is to feel the sun from both sides.
— *David Viscott*

'Tis better to have loved and lost
Than never to have loved at all.
— *Alfred, Lord Tennyson*

To fall in love is to create a religion that has a fallible god.
— *Jorge Luis Borges*

Love is the triumph of imagination over intelligence.
— *H. L. Mencken*

Intimate relationships cannot substitute for a life plan. But to have any meaning or viability at all, a life plan must include intimate relationships. — *Harriet Lerner*

I was born when you kissed me. I died when you left me. I lived a few weeks while you loved me.

— HUMPHREY BOGART

Oh, life is a glorious cycle of song,
A medley of extemporanea;
And love is a thing that can never go wrong;
And I am Marie of Romania.

— Dorothy Parker

In love, one and one are one.

—Jean-Paul Sartre

A man is already halfway in love with any woman who
listens to him. *— Brendan Francis*

Every instance of heartbreak can teach us powerful lessons
about creating the kind of love we really want.

— Martha Beck

The best proof of love is trust.

—Joyce Brothers

We love because it's the only true adventure.

— Nikki Giovanni

Don't brood. Get on with living and loving. You don't have
forever. *— Leo Buscaglia*

Love is said to be blind, but I know some fellows in love who
can see twice as much in their sweethearts as I do.

—Josh Billings

I am certainly not an authority on love because there are no
authorities on love, just those who've had luck with it and
those who haven't.

— Bill Cosby

Love is metaphysical gravity.

— R. Buckminster Fuller

The great question that has never been answered, and which I have not yet been able to answer, despite my 30 years of research into the feminine soul, is "What does a woman want?"

— *Sigmund Freud*

Love is a perky elf dancing a merry little jig and then suddenly he turns on you with a miniature machine gun.

— *Matt Groening*

Men are not the enemy, but the fellow victims. The real enemy is women's denigration of themselves.

— *Betty Friedan*

The mark of a true crush...is that you fall in love first and grope for reasons afterward. — *Shana Alexander*

Men and women belong to different species and communications between them is still in its infancy. — *Bill Cosby*

There is love of course. And then there's life, its enemy.

—*Jean Anouilh*

A man never knows how to say good-bye; a woman never knows when to say it. — *Helen Rowland*

When you realize you want to spend the rest of your life with somebody, you want the rest of your life to start as soon as possible. — *Billy Crystal*

Women want mediocre men, and men are working hard to become as mediocre as possible. — *Margaret Mead*

There are three things men can do with women: love them, suffer for them, or turn them into literature. — *Stephen Stills*

Can you imagine a world without men? No crime and lots of happy fat women. — *Nicole Hollander*

One is very crazy when in love.

— *Sigmund Freud*

There is one thing I would break up over and that is if she caught me with another woman. I wouldn't stand for that.

— *Steve Martin*

There is no reciprocity. Men love women, women love children, children love hamsters.

— *Alice Thomas Ellis*

The formula for achieving a successful relationship is simple: you should treat all disasters as if they were trivialities but never treat a triviality as if it were a disaster.

— *Quentin Crisp*

Nature gives you the face you have at 20; it is up to you to merit the face you have at 50.

— *Coco Chanel*

I don't believe man is a woman's natural enemy. Perhaps his lawyer is.

— *Shana Alexander*

The only creatures that are evolved enough to convey pure love are dogs and infants.

—*Johnny Depp*

The entire sum of existence is the magic of being needed by just one other person.

— *Vi Putnam*

We cannot really love anybody with whom we never laugh.

— *Agnes Repplier*

It is a curious thought, but it is only when you see people looking ridiculous that you realize just how much you love them.

— *Agatha Christie*

Passion is the quickest to develop, and the quickest to fade. Intimacy develops more slowly, and commitment more gradually still.

— *Robert Sternberg*

Love is a fire. But whether it is going to warm your hearth or burn down your house, you can never tell.
— *Joan Crawford*

Love builds bridges where there are none.
— *R. H. Delaney*

Intimacy is being seen and known as the person you truly are.
— *Amy Bloom*

Men want the same thing from their underwear that they want from women: a little bit of support, and a little bit of freedom.
— *Jerry Seinfeld*

It is not love that is blind, but jealousy.
— *Lawrence Durrell*

I don't want to live. I want to love first and live incidentally.
— *Zelda Fitzgerald*

You never lose by loving. You always lose by holding back.
— *Barbara De Angelis*

The heart of another is a dark forest, always, no matter how close it has been to one's own.
— *Willa Cather*

Marriage

My wife and I were happy for 20 years. Then we met.
— *Rodney Dangerfield*

'Tis more blessed to give than receive; for example, wedding presents.
— *H. L. Mencken*

The best way to get husbands to do something is to suggest that perhaps they are too old to do it.
— *Shirley MacLaine*

The value of marriage is not that adults produce children but that children produce adults.
— *Peter De Vries*

He taught me housekeeping; when I divorce I keep the house.
— *Zsa Zsa Gabor*

A happy marriage is the world's best bargain.
— *O. A. Battista*

I know you've been married to the same woman for 69 years. That is marvelous. It must be very inexpensive.
— *Johnny Carson*

There is more to marriage than four bare legs under a blanket.
— *Robertson Davies*

The majority of husbands remind me of an orangutan trying to play the violin.
— *Honoré de Balzac*

It's not a good idea to put your wife into a novel; not your latest wife anyway.
— *Norman Mailer*

What do I know about sex? I'm a married man.
— *Tom Clancy*

Intimacy is what makes a marriage, not a ceremony, not a piece of paper from the state.
— *Kathleen Norris*

Always get married early in the morning. That way, if it doesn't work out, you haven't wasted a whole day.
— *Mickey Rooney*

Marriage is about the most expensive way for the average
man to get laundry done.   — *Burt Reynolds*

The married are those who have taken the terrible risk of
intimacy and, having taken it, know life without intimacy to
be impossible.   — *Carolyn Heilbrun*

Marriage is not a noun; it's a verb. It isn't something you get.
It's something you do. It's the way you love your partner
every day.   — *Barbara De Angelis*

A successful marriage requires falling in love many times,
always with the same person.   — *Mignon McLaughlin*

"I am" is reportedly the shortest sentence in the English
language. Could it be that "I do" is the longest sentence?
                                              — *George Carlin*

My advice to you is get married: if you find a good wife
you'll be happy; if not, you'll become a philosopher.
                                              — *Socrates*

One has to be able to count if only so that at 50 one doesn't
marry a girl of 20.   — *Maxim Gorky*

I believe in the institution of marriage, and I intend to keep
trying till I get it right.   — *Richard Pryor*

I'd marry again if I found a man who had
fifteen million dollars, would sign over half
to me, and guarantee that he'd be dead
within a year.

— BETTE DAVIS

A great marriage is not when the "perfect couple" comes together. It is when an imperfect couple learns to enjoy their differences.
— *Dave Meurer*

Nobody wants to be married to a doctor who works weekends and makes house calls at two a.m. But every patient would like to find one.
— *Ellen Goodman*

In every marriage more than a week old, there are grounds for divorce. The trick is to find, and continue to find, grounds for marriage.
— *Robert Anderson*

I used to believe that marriage would diminish me, reduce my options. That you had to be someone less to live with someone else when, of course, you have to be someone more.
— *Candice Bergen*

Most wives think of their husbands as bumbling braggarts with whom they happen to be in love.
— *Jackie Gleason*

For marriage to be a success, every woman and every man should have her and his own bathroom. The end.
— *Catherine Zeta-Jones*

Keep your eyes wide open before marriage, half shut afterwards.
— *Benjamin Franklin*

Almost no one is foolish enough to imagine that he automatically deserves great success in any field of activity; yet almost everyone believes that he automatically deserves success in marriage.
— *Sydney J. Harris*

A good marriage would be between a blind wife and a deaf husband.
— *Honoré de Balzac*

If variety is the spice of life, marriage is the big can of leftover Spam.
— *Johnny Carson*

Marriage has no guarantees. If that's what you're looking for, go live with a car battery.
— *Erma Bombeck*

If men knew how women pass the time when they are alone, they'd never marry.
— *O. Henry*

It seemed to me that the desire to get married—which, I regret to say, I believe is basic and primal in women—is followed almost immediately by an equally basic and primal urge—which is to be single again.
— *Nora Ephron*

I married beneath me, all women do.
— *Nancy Astor*

My toughest fight was with my first wife.
— *Muhammad Ali*

All men make mistakes, but married men find out about them sooner.
— *Red Skelton*

Half a loafer is better than no husband at all.
— *Louis Safian*

An archaeologist is the best husband a woman can have; the older she gets the more interested he is in her.
— *Agatha Christie*

Husbands are like fires—they go out when unattended.
— *Zsa Zsa Gabor*

I don't think I'll get married again. I'll just find a woman I don't like and give her a house.
— *Lewis Grizzard*

For a while we pondered whether to take a vacation or get a divorce. We decided that a trip to Bermuda is over in two weeks, but a divorce is something you always have.
— *Woody Allen*

In Hollywood, an equitable divorce settlement means each party getting 50 percent of publicity.   — *Lauren Bacall*

Don't forget Mother's Day. Or as they call it in Beverly Hills, Dad's Third Wife Day.   — *Jay Leno*

I have often wanted to drown my troubles, but I can't get my wife to go swimming.   — *Jimmy Carter*

Parenthood

We spend the first 12 months of our children's lives teaching them to walk and talk, and the next 12 years telling them to sit down and shut up.   — *Phyllis Diller*

Giving birth is like taking your lower lip and forcing it over your head.   — *Carol Burnett*

There are two things in life for which we are never truly prepared: twins.   — *Josh Billings*

Children have never been very good at listening to their elders, but they have never failed to imitate them.

— *James Baldwin*

Onion rings in the car cushions do not improve with time.

— *Erma Bombeck*

Outings are so much more fun when we can savor them through the children's eyes.   — *Lawana Blackwell*

I want my children to have all the things I couldn't afford.
Then I want to move in with them.   **Phyllis Diller**

Ask your child what he wants for dinner only if he's buying.
                                          — *Fran Lebowitz*

Motherhood is a wonderful thing—what a pity to waste it
on children.   —*Judith Pugh*

Grown-ups never understand anything for themselves, and it
is tiresome for children to be always and forever explaining
things to them.   — *Antoine de Saint-Exupéry*

A king, realizing his incompetence, can either delegate or
abdicate his duties. A father can do neither. If only sons could
see the paradox, they would understand the dilemma.
                                          — *Marlene Dietrich*

Nothing you do for children is ever wasted. They seem not
to notice us, hovering, averting our eyes, and they seldom
offer thanks, but what we do for them is never wasted.
                                          — *Garrison Keillor*

Tired mothers find that spanking takes less time than reason-
ing and penetrates sooner to the seat of the memory.
                                          — *Will Durant*

If evolution really works, how come mothers only have two
hands?   — *Milton Berle*

Never raise your hand to your kids. It leaves your groin
unprotected.   — *Red Buttons*

Always end the name of your child with a vowel, so that
when you yell the name will carry.   — *Bill Cosby*

Live so that when your children think of fairness and integrity,
they think of you.   — *H. Jackson Brown, Jr.*

Douglas Adams

Universal Humor

Not many people get to blow up Earth and then enjoy a fabulous literary career. But that's how it started for Douglas Adams, the British creator of *The Hitchhiker's Guide to the Galaxy.*

When he was just 26, the BBC began broadcasting his tale about a young man who roves among the stars after his planet has been destroyed to make way for an intergalactic highway. 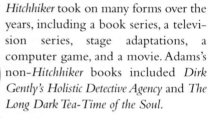 *Hitchhiker* took on many forms over the years, including a book series, a television series, stage adaptations, a computer game, and a movie. Adams's non-*Hitchhiker* books included *Dirk Gently's Holistic Detective Agency* and *The Long Dark Tea-Time of the Soul.*

Adams showed a particular fondness for wildlife in both his fiction and nonfiction. He also relished skewering the planet's most peculiar species, *Homo sapiens,* with his unique brand of absurdist wit.

Adams himself unexpectedly departed this world in 2001, dying of a heart attack at age 49.

*

All it takes to fly is to hurl yourself at the ground...and miss.

*

People complain that there's a lot of rubbish online, or that it's dominated by Americans, or that you can't necessarily trust what you read on the Web. Imagine trying to apply any of those criticisms to what you hear on the telephone. Of course you can't "trust" what people tell you on the Web any more than you can "trust" what people tell you on megaphones, postcards or in restaurants.

*

My absolute favorite piece of information is the fact that young sloths are so inept that they frequently grab their own arms and legs instead of tree limbs, and fall out of trees.

*

There is a theory which states that if ever anybody discovers exactly what the Universe is for and why it is here, it will instantly disappear and be replaced by something even more bizarre and inexplicable. There is another theory which states that this has already happened.

*

Human beings, who are almost unique in having the ability to learn from the experience of others, are also remarkable for their apparent disinclination to do so.

*

Anything that is in the world when you're born is normal and ordinary and is just part of the way the world works. Anything that's invented between when you're 15 and 35 is new and exciting and revolutionary and you can probably get a career in it. Anything invented after you're 35 is against the natural order of things.

*

I really didn't foresee the Internet. But then, neither did the computer industry. Not that that tells us very much, of course— the computer industry didn't even foresee that the century was going to end.

41

It is very important that children learn from their fathers and mothers how to love one another— not in the school, not from the teacher, but from you. It is very important that you share with your children the joy of that smile. There will be misunderstandings; every family has its cross, its suffering. Always be the first to forgive with a smile. Be cheerful, be happy.

— *Mother Teresa*

If you bungle raising your children, I don't think whatever else you do matters very much.

— *Jackie Kennedy Onassis*

If you have never been hated by your child, you have never been a parent.

— *Bette Davis*

There was a time when we expected nothing of our children but obedience, as opposed to the present, when we expect everything of them but obedience.

— *Anatole Broyard*

A child who is allowed to be disrespectful to his parents will not have true respect for anyone.

— *Billy Graham*

When I was a kid my parents moved a lot, but I always found them.

— *Rodney Dangerfield*

I take my children everywhere, but they always find their way back home.

— *Robert Orben*

There is no such thing as "fun for the whole family."

— *Jerry Seinfeld*

I have found the best way to give advice to your children is to find out what they want and then advise them to do it.

— *Harry S. Truman*

The best way to keep children at home is to make the home atmosphere pleasant—and let the air out of the tires.

— *Dorothy Parker*

If your parents never had children, chances are you won't either. — *Dick Cavett*

Always be nice to those younger than you, because they are the ones who will be writing about you. — *Cyril Connolly*

Always be nice to your children because they are the ones who will choose your rest home. — *Phyllis Diller*

No matter how many communes anybody invents, the family always creeps back. — *Margaret Mead*

If a woman has to choose between catching a fly ball and saving an infant's life, she will choose to save the infant's life without even considering if there is a man on base. — *Dave Barry*

We should never permit ourselves to do anything that we are not willing to see our children do. — *Brigham Young*

The emotional, sexual, and psychological stereotyping of females begins when the doctor says, "It's a girl." — *Shirley Chisholm*

Human beings are the only creatures on earth that allow their children to come back home. — *Bill Cosby*

A baseball manager has learned a lot about his job from having played the game, but a parent has not learned a thing from having once been a child. — *Bill Cosby*

Because I am a mother, I am capable of being shocked: as I never was when I was not one. — *Margaret Atwood*

Watching your daughter being collected by her date feels like handing over a million-dollar Stradivarius to a gorilla. — *Jim Bishop*

Setting a good example for children takes all the fun out of middle age.
— *William Feather*

Having children makes you no more a parent than having a piano makes you a pianist.
— *Michael Levine*

Aging

My parents didn't want to move to Florida, but they turned 60 and that's the law.
—*Jerry Seinfeld*

Age is a question of mind over matter. If you don't mind, it doesn't matter.
— *Satchel Paige*

All would live long, but none would be old.
— *Benjamin Franklin*

Age is a high price to pay for maturity.
— *Tom Stoppard*

Each has his past shut in him like the leaves of a book known to him by heart and his friends can only read the title.
— *Virginia Woolf*

Beautiful young people are accidents of nature, but beautiful old people are works of art.
— *Eleanor Roosevelt*

The secret of staying young is to live honestly, eat slowly, and lie about your age.
— *Lucille Ball*

Men do not quit playing because they grow old; they grow old because they quit playing. — *Oliver Wendell Holmes*

While there's snow on the roof, it doesn't mean the fire has gone out in the furnace. — *John G. Diefenbaker*

Men become much more attractive when they start looking older. But it doesn't do much for women, though we do have an advantage: makeup. — *Bette Davis*

And in the end, it's not the years in your life that count. It's the life in your years. — *Abraham Lincoln*

You're only as young as the last time you changed your mind. — *Timothy Leary*

I wasted time, and now doth time waste me. — *William Shakespeare*

There's nothing worse than being an aging young person. — *Richard Pryor*

There is still no cure for the common birthday. — *John Glenn*

My doctor recently told me that jogging could add years to my life. I think he was right. I feel 10 years older already. — *Milton Berle*

Time goes by: Reputation increases, ability declines. — *Dag Hammarskjöld*

First you forget names, then you forget faces. Next you forget to pull your zipper up and finally, you forget to pull it down. — *George Burns*

Old age is like everything else. To make a success of it, you've got to start young. — *Fred Astaire*

I think it would be interesting if old people got anti-Alzheimer's disease where they slowly began to recover other people's lost memories.

— George Carlin

If wrinkles must be written upon our brows, let them not be written upon the heart. The spirit should never grow old.

—John Kenneth Galbraith

I'll see a beautiful girl walking up to me and I'll think, Oh, my God, I can't believe my good luck. But then she'll say, "Where's your son?" or "My mother loves you."

— James Caan

You know you're getting old when all the names in your black book have M.D. after them.

— Arnold Palmer

It is not all bad, this getting old, ripening. After the fruit has got its growth it should juice up and mellow. God forbid I should live long enough to ferment and rot and fall to the ground in a squash.

—Josh Billings

Cherish all your happy moments: they make a fine cushion for old age.

— Christopher Morley

It's no longer a question of staying healthy. It's a question of finding a sickness you like.

—Jackie Mason

I refuse to admit that I am more than 52, even if that does make my sons illegitimate.

— Nancy Astor

A legend is an old man with a cane known for what he used to do. I'm still doing it.

— Miles Davis

Age is no guarantee of maturity.

— LAWANA BLACKWELL

THE PATH THROUGH LIFE

To me, old age is always 15 years older than I am.

— *Bernard M. Baruch*

Age is not important unless you're a cheese.

— *Helen Hayes*

I don't have false teeth. Do you think I'd buy teeth like these?

— *Carol Burnett*

One of the good things about getting older is you find you're more interesting than most of the people you meet.

— *Lee Marvin*

Another belief of mine: that everyone else my age is an adult, whereas I am merely in disguise.   — *Margaret Atwood*

It is very strange that the years teach us patience—that the shorter our time, the greater our capacity for waiting.

— *Elizabeth Taylor*

Forty is the old age of youth;
50 is the youth of old age.   — *Victor Hugo*

Beware of the young doctor and the old barber.

— *Benjamin Franklin*

You can't reach old age by another man's road. My habits protect my life but they would assassinate you.

— *Mark Twain*

Time sneaks up on you like a windshield on a bug.

—*John Lithgow*

You can judge your age by the amount of pain you feel when you come in contact with a new idea.   — *Pearl S. Buck*

I look better, feel better, make love better and I'll tell you something else...I never lied better.   — *George Burns*

The dead might as well try to speak to the living as the old to the young.
— *Willa Cather*

To keep the heart unwrinkled, to be hopeful, kindly, cheerful, reverent—that is to triumph over old age.
— *Thomas Bailey Aldrich*

Gray hair is God's graffiti.
— *Bill Cosby*

Life is a moderately good play with a badly written third act.
— *Truman Capote*

You know you're getting old when you get that one candle on the cake. It's like, "See if you can blow this out."
— *Jerry Seinfeld*

You know you're getting old when you've got money to burn, but the fire's gone out.
— *Hy Gardner*

I have a problem about being nearly 60: I keep waking up in the morning and thinking I'm 31.
— *Elizabeth Janeway*

When I was young I was called a rugged individualist. When I was in my 50s I was considered eccentric. Here I am doing and saying the same things I did then and I'm labeled senile.

— GEORGE BURNS

My grandmother started walking five miles a day when she was 60. She's 97 now, and we don't know where the hell she is.
— *Ellen DeGeneres*

THE PATH THROUGH LIFE

How old would you be if you didn't know how old you are?

— Satchel Paige

I used to dread getting older because I thought I would not be able to do all the things I wanted to do, but now that I am older I find that I don't want to do them.

— Nancy Astor

If you live long enough, the venerability factor creeps in; first, you get accused of things you never did, and later, credited for virtues you never had.

— I. F. Stone

Men should think twice before making widowhood women's only path to power.

— Gloria Steinem

A man who correctly guesses a woman's age may be smart, but he's not very bright.

— Lucille Ball

A man is not old until regrets take the place of dreams.

—John Barrymore

At my age flowers scare me.

— George Burns

Of all the self-fulfilling prophecies in our culture, the assumption that aging means decline and poor health is probably the deadliest.

— Marilyn Ferguson

You must have been warned against letting the golden hours slip by; but some of them are golden only because we let them slip by.

—James M. Barrie

When doctors and undertakers meet, they always wink at each other.

— W. C. Fields

Health nuts are going to feel stupid someday, lying in hospitals dying of nothing.

— Redd Foxx

Death

Like everyone else who makes the mistake of getting older,
I begin each day with coffee and obituaries.   — *Bill Cosby*

On the plus side, death is one of the few things that can be
done as easily lying down.   — *Woody Allen*

He's so old that when he orders a three-minute egg, they ask
for the money up front.   — *Milton Berle*

My doctor gave me six months to live, but when I couldn't
pay the bill he gave me six months more.   — *Walter Matthau*

I look upon life as a gift from God. I did nothing to earn it.
Now that the time is coming to give it back, I have no right
to complain.   — *Joyce Cary*

It is a sobering thought that when Mozart was my age, he
had been dead for two years.   — *Tom Lehrer*

Frisbeetarianism is the belief that when you die, your soul
goes up on the roof and gets stuck.   — *George Carlin*

Desire is half of life; indifference is half of death.
                                                  — *Kahlil Gibran*

Nothing dies harder than a bad idea.
                                                  — *Julia Cameron*

Once you're dead you're made for life.
                                                  — *Jimi Hendrix*

When I stand before God at the end of my life, I would hope that I would not have a single bit of talent left, and could say, "I used everything you gave me."

— *Erma Bombeck*

I submit to you that if a man hasn't discovered something he will die for, he isn't fit to live. — *Martin Luther King, Jr.*

Do not fear death so much, but rather the inadequate life.

— *Bertolt Brecht*

If life was fair, Elvis would be alive and all the impersonators would be dead. — *Johnny Carson*

They say such nice things about people at their funerals that it makes me sad that I'm going to miss mine by just a few days.

— *Garrison Keillor*

Death is caused by swallowing small amounts of saliva over a long period of time. — *George Carlin*

Death ends a life, not a relationship.

— JACK LEMMON

Our brains are 70-year clocks. The Angel of Life winds them up once for all, then closes the case, and gives the key into the hand of the Angel of the Resurrection.

— *Oliver Wendell Holmes*

I detest life-insurance agents; they always argue that I shall some day die, which is not so. — *Stephen Leacock*

Why are our days numbered and not, say, lettered?

— *Woody Allen*

In the city a funeral is just an interruption of traffic; in the country it is a form of popular entertainment.

— *George Ade*

I'm always relieved when someone is delivering a eulogy and I realize I'm listening to it.   — *George Carlin*

I am dying from the treatment of too many physicians.

— *Alexander the Great*

If the doctor told me I had only six minutes to live, I'd type a little faster.   — *Isaac Asimov*

His death was the first time that Ed Wynn ever made anyone sad.   — *Red Skelton*

That would be a good thing for them to cut on my tombstone: Wherever she went, including here, it was against her better judgment.   — *Dorothy Parker*

That's all a man can hope for during his lifetime—to set an example—and when he is dead, to be an inspiration for history.

— *William McKinley*

Immortality is a long shot, I admit. But somebody has to be first.   — *Bill Cosby*

If you live to be 100, you've got it made. Very few people die past that age.   — *George Burns*

If I could drop dead right now, I'd be the happiest man alive.

— *Samuel Goldwyn*

Dying is a very dull, dreary affair. And my advice to you is to have nothing whatever to do with it.

— *W. Somerset Maugham*

A cynic is a man who, when he smells flowers, looks around for a coffin.
H. L. Mencken

He is one of those people who would be enormously improved by death.
— Saki

There is no such thing as bad publicity except your own obituary.
— Brendan Behan

Death is nothing, but to live defeated and inglorious is to die daily.
— Napoleon Bonaparte

If physical death is the price that I must pay to free my white brothers and sisters from a permanent death of the spirit, then nothing can be more redemptive.
— Martin Luther King, Jr.

What I look forward to is continued immaturity followed by death.
— Dave Barry

I do not believe that any man fears to be dead, but only the stroke of death.
— Francis Bacon

When I die, if the word *thong* appears in the first or second sentence of my obituary, I've screwed up.
— Albert Brooks

I'm the one that has to die when it's time for me to die, so let me live my life, the way I want to.
—Jimi Hendrix

There are some days when I think I'm going to die from an overdose of satisfaction.
— Salvador Dalí

Let us endeavor so to live that when we come to die even the undertaker will be sorry.
— Mark Twain

Suicide is a permanent solution to a temporary problem.
— Phil Donahue

The bitterest tears shed over graves are for words left unsaid and deeds left undone.
— *Harriet Beecher Stowe*

An autobiography is an obituary in serial form with the last installment missing.
— *Quentin Crisp*

My friends are my estate.
— *Emily Dickinson*

Any man who has $10,000 left when he dies is a failure.
— *Errol Flynn*

Death is a challenge. It tells us not to waste time.... It tells us to tell each other right now that we love each other.
— *Leo Buscaglia*

You don't die in the United States, you underachieve.
— *Jerzy Kosinski*

I have never killed a man, but I have read many obituaries with a lot of pleasure.
— *Clarence Darrow*

Truth sits upon the lips of dying men.
— *Matthew Arnold*

Do not go gentle into that good night
Old age should burn and rave at close of day;
Rage, rage against the dying of the light.
— *Dylan Thomas*

Life is pleasant. Death is peaceful.
It's the transition that's troublesome.
— *Isaac Asimov*

Death is not the end. There remains the litigation over the estate.
— *Ambrose Bierce*

Life is tragic simply because the earth turns and the sun inexorably rises and sets, and one day, for each of us, the sun will go down for the last, last time. *—James Baldwin*

The thinker dies, but his thoughts are beyond the reach of destruction. Men are mortal; but ideas are immortal.
— Richard Adams

Life is hardly more than a fraction of a second. Such a little time to prepare oneself for eternity! *— Paul Gauguin*

To die will be an awfully big adventure.
—James M. Barrie

I don't believe in dying. It's been done. I'm working on a new exit. Besides, I can't die now—I'm booked.
— George Burns

Death will be a great relief. No more interviews.
— Katharine Hepburn

When you are about to die, a wombat is better than no company at all. *— Roger Zelazny*

Always go to other people's funerals; otherwise they won't come to yours.

—YOGI BERRA

Last Words

When the Grim Reaper signals you to make your final exit from the world stage, how well will you perform? Will you have the presence of mind to summon up an inspired line or two? Here's a collection of several famous people's last words— some touching, some ironic, and a few downright funny.

The ladies have to go first. Get in the lifeboat, to please me. Good-bye, dearie. I'll see you later.

— John Jacob Astor IV, aboard the *Titanic*

Codeine...bourbon. — Tallulah Bankhead

How were the receipts today at Madison Square Garden?

— P. T. Barnum

Friends applaud, the comedy is finished. — Ludwig van Beethoven

I should never have switched from Scotch to martinis.

— Humphrey Bogart

That was the best ice-cream soda I ever tasted. — Lou Costello

That was a great game of golf, fellers. — Bing Crosby

I am not the least afraid to die. — Charles Darwin

The fog is rising. — Emily Dickinson

KHAQQ calling Itasca. We must be on you, but cannot see you. Gas is running low. — Amelia Earhart

I've never felt better. — Douglas Fairbanks, Sr.

I've had a hell of a lot of fun and I've enjoyed every minute of it. — Errol Flynn

Turn up the lights. I don't want to go home in the dark. — O. Henry

Leave the shower curtain on the inside of the tub. — Conrad N. Hilton

Go on, get out—last words are for fools who haven't said enough. — Karl Marx

I am just going outside and may be some time. — Lawrence Oates, Antarctic expedition, 1912

You can keep the things of bronze and stone and give me one man to remember me just once a year. — Damon Runyon

Drink to me. — Pablo Picasso

Everybody has got to die, but I have always believed an exception would be made in my case. Now what? — William Saroyan

They couldn't hit an elephant at this dist—. — John Sedgwick, Union Civil War general

I have offended God and mankind because my work did not reach the quality it should have. — Leonardo da Vinci

Either that wallpaper goes, or I do. — Oscar Wilde

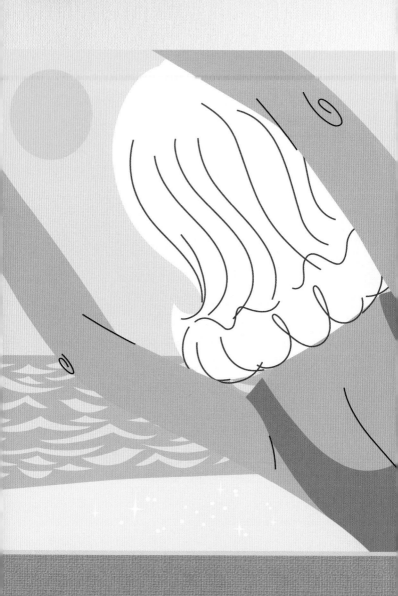

2

The Human **Spirit**

Okay, let's go deeper now. The subject for the quotations in this part is nothing less profound than religion, the meaning of life, and our own particular places within humanity and the world.

Faith

We trust, sir, that God is on our side. It is more important to know that we are on God's side. — *Abraham Lincoln*

One, on God's side, is a majority. — *Wendell Phillips*

I do not feel obliged to believe that the same God who has endowed us with sense, reason, and intellect has intended us to forgo their use. — *Galileo*

Science without religion is lame, religion without science is blind. — *Albert Einstein*

Beware when the great God lets loose a thinker on this planet. — *Ralph Waldo Emerson*

There is no question that there is an unseen world. The problem is, how far is it from midtown and how late is it open? — *Woody Allen*

Treat the other man's faith gently; it is all he has to believe with. His mind was created for his own thoughts, not yours or mine. — *Henry S. Haskins*

We must respect the other fellow's religion, but only in the sense and to the extent that we respect his theory that his wife is beautiful and his children smart. — *H. L. Mencken*

This only is denied to God: the power to undo the past. — *Agathon*

I have an everyday religion that works for me. Love yourself first, and everything else falls into line. You really have to love yourself to get anything done in this world. — *Lucille Ball*

Can you see the holiness in those things you take for granted —a paved road or a washing machine? If you concentrate on finding what is good in every situation, you will discover that your life will suddenly be filled with gratitude, a feeling that nurtures the soul. — *Harold S. Kushner*

You ask: What is the meaning or purpose of life? I can only answer with another question: Do you think we are wise enough to read God's mind? — *Freeman Dyson*

God grant me the serenity to accept the things I cannot change, the courage to change the things I can, and the wisdom to know the difference. — *Reinhold Niebuhr*

Faith is taking the first step even when you don't see the whole staircase. — *Martin Luther King, Jr.*

There's nothing written in the Bible, Old or New Testament, that says, "If you believe in Me, you ain't going to have no troubles." — *Ray Charles*

Holiness is not the luxury of a few. It is everyone's duty, yours and mine. — *Mother Teresa*

Every charitable act is a stepping stone toward heaven. — *Henry Ward Beecher*

What is faith worth if it is not translated into action? — *Mahatma Gandhi*

The gods help them that help themselves.

— *Aesop*

If God can work through me, he can work through anyone.

— *Saint Francis of Assisi*

We're here for a reason. I believe a bit of the reason is to throw little torches out to lead people through the dark.

— *Whoopi Goldberg*

As far as we can discern, the sole purpose of human existence is to kindle a light in the darkness of mere being.

— *Carl Jung*

The fact that I can plant a seed and it becomes a flower, share a bit of knowledge and it becomes another's, smile at someone and receive a smile in return, are to me continual spiritual exercises.

— *Leo Buscaglia*

God is not a cosmic bellboy for whom we can press a button to get things done.

— *Harry Emerson Fosdick*

God made Truth with many doors to welcome every believer who knocks on them.

— *Kahlil Gibran*

In the name of God, stop a moment, cease your work, look around you.

— *Leo Tolstoy*

Religion is what keeps the poor from murdering the rich.

— NAPOLEON BONAPARTE

It's faith in something and enthusiasm for something that makes life worth living.

— *Oliver Wendell Holmes*

The devil can cite Scripture for his purpose.

— *William Shakespeare*

THE HUMAN SPIRIT

There is no need to go to India or anywhere else to find peace. You will find that deep place of silence right in your room, your garden or even your bathtub.

— *Elisabeth Kubler-Ross*

I conceive the essential task of religion to be "to develop the consciences, the ideals, and the aspirations of mankind."

— *Robert Millikan*

I think vital religion has always suffered when orthodoxy is more regarded than virtue. The scriptures assure me that at the last day we shall not be examined on what we thought but what we did.

— *Benjamin Franklin*

The belief in a supernatural source of evil is not necessary; men alone are quite capable of every wickedness.

— *Joseph Conrad*

Believe those who are seeking the truth; doubt those who find it.

— *André Gide*

Say not, "I have found the truth," but rather, "I have found a truth."

— *Kahlil Gibran*

Say nothing of my religion. It is known to God and myself alone. Its evidence before the world is to be sought in my life: if it has been honest and dutiful to society, the religion which has regulated it cannot be a bad one.

— *Thomas Jefferson*

Faith moves mountains, but you have to keep pushing while you are praying.

— *Mason Cooley*

Pray as if everything depended upon God and work as if everything depended upon man.

— *Francis Cardinal Spellman*

Earth's crammed with heaven,
And every common bush afire with God;
But only he who sees, takes off his shoes;
The rest sit round it and pluck blackberries.

— *Elizabeth Barrett Browning*

Character is what God and the angels know of us; reputation is what men and women think of us.   — *Horace Mann*

An honest man is the noblest work of God.

— *Alexander Pope*

The wish to pray is a prayer in itself. God can ask no more than that of us.   — *Georges Bernanos*

The time to pray is not when we are in a tight spot but just as soon as we get out of it.   — *Josh Billings*

God moves in a mysterious way His wonders to perform.

— *William Cowper*

The Lord had the wonderful advantage of being able to work alone.   — *Kofi Annan*

Sooner or later ... you are going to be looking at God saying, "We're going to be lucky if we get out of here." Your life is going to be in front of you and then you are going to realize that you'd rather be grocery shopping.

— *Ed Barry*

Yesterday is history, tomorrow is a mystery, today is God's gift, that's why we call it the present.   — *Joan Rivers*

My religion is very simple. My religion is kindness.

— *The Dalai Lama*

We are always on the anvil; by trials God is shaping us for higher things.   — *Henry Ward Beecher*

It is difficult to make a man miserable while he feels worthy of himself and claims kindred to the great God who made him. — *Abraham Lincoln*

We have just enough religion to make us hate, but not enough to make us love one another. — *Jonathan Swift*

Sometimes you struggle so hard to feed your family one way, you forget to feed them the other way, with spiritual nourishment. Everybody needs that. — *James Brown*

Every religion is true one way or another. It is true when understood metaphorically. But when it gets stuck in its own metaphors, interpreting them as facts, then you are in trouble. — *Joseph Campbell*

Practically speaking, your religion is the story you tell about your life. — *Andrew Greeley*

Coincidences are spiritual puns. — *G. K. Chesterton*

I personally believe that each of us was put here for a purpose—to build, not to destroy. If I can make people smile, then I have served my purpose for God. — *Red Skelton*

If only God would give me some clear sign!
Like making a large deposit in my name
at a Swiss bank.

— WOODY ALLEN

There are two ways to live: you can live as if nothing is a miracle; you can live as if everything is a miracle. — *Albert Einstein*

God gives us relatives; thank God we can choose our friends.

— *Ethel Mumford*

I am determined that my children shall be brought up in their father's religion, if they can find out what it is.

— *Charles Lamb*

In the beginning there was nothing. God said, "Let there be light!" And there was light. There was still nothing, but you could see it a whole lot better. — *Ellen DeGeneres*

I have as much authority as the Pope—I just don't have as many people who believe it. — *George Carlin*

See everything; overlook a great deal; correct a little.

— *Pope John XXIII*

Making Sense of It All

Realize deeply that the present moment is all you ever have.

— *Eckhart Tolle*

Hope is only the love of life.

— *Henri-Frédéric Amiel*

Hope begins in the dark, the stubborn hope that if you just show up and try to do the right thing, the dawn will come. You wait and watch and work: You don't give up.

— *Anne Lamott*

Few people even scratch the surface, much less exhaust the contemplation of their own experience.   — *Randolph Bourne*

I happen to feel that the degree of a person's intelligence is directly reflected by the number of conflicting attitudes she can bring to bear on the same topic.   — *Lisa Alther*

The way I see it, if you want the rainbow, you gotta put up with the rain.   — *Dolly Parton*

Life is like an ever-shifting kaleidoscope—a slight change, and all patterns alter.   — *Susan Salzberg*

If you are going to ask yourself life-changing questions, be sure to do something with the answers.   — *Bo Bennett*

Those who dream by day are cognizant of many things which escape those who dream only by night.   — *Edgar Allan Poe*

It is said an eastern monarch once charged his wise men to invent a sentence, to be ever in view, and which should be true and appropriate in all times and situations. They presented him with the words, "And this, too, shall pass away." How much it expresses! How chastening in the hour of pride! How consoling in the depths of affliction!

— *Abraham Lincoln*

Most things get better by themselves. Most things, in fact, are better by morning.   — *Lewis Thomas*

Things in life will not always run smoothly. Sometimes we will be rising toward the heights—then all will seem to reverse itself and start downward. The great fact to remember is that the trend of civilization itself is forever upward, that a line drawn through the middle of the peaks and the valleys of the centuries always has an upward trend.

— *Endicott Peabody*

Life's a voyage that's homeward bound.

— *Herman Melville*

Learning to live what you're born with is the process, the involvement, the making of a life. — *Diane Wakoski*

We are here to add what we can to life, not to get what we can from it. — *William Osler*

Life isn't fair. It's just fairer than death, that's all.

— *William Goldman*

We would often be sorry if our wishes were gratified.

— *Aesop*

Wisdom consists of the anticipation of consequences.

— *Norman Cousins*

In order to be walked on, you have to be lying down.

— *Brian Weir*

Experience is a hard teacher because she gives the test first, the lesson afterwards. — *Vernon Sanders Law*

It is our choices ... that show what we truly are, far more than our abilities. — *J. K. Rowling*

Everything you can imagine is real.

— *Pablo Picasso*

There are really only three types of people: those who make things happen, those who watch things happen, and those who say, "What happened?"

— ANN LANDERS

THE HUMAN SPIRIT

We grow great by dreams. All big men are dreamers.

— *Woodrow Wilson*

All that counts in life is intention.

— *Andrea Bocelli*

You and I are essentially infinite choice-makers. In every moment of our existence, we are in that field of all possibilities where we have access to an infinity of choices.

— *Deepak Chopra*

We don't see things as they are, we see them as *we* are.

— *Anaïs Nin*

Self-esteem is the reputation we acquire with ourselves.

— *Nathaniel Branden*

No one can make you feel inferior without your consent.

— *Eleanor Roosevelt*

Vanity and pride are different things, though the words are often used synonymously. A person may be proud without being vain. Pride relates more to our opinion of ourselves, vanity to what we would have others think of us.

— *Jane Austen*

Every problem has a gift for you in its hands.

— *Richard Bach*

If a problem has no solution, it may not be a problem, but a fact—not to be solved, but to be coped with over time.

— *Shimon Peres*

All generalizations are dangerous, even this one.

— *Alexandre Dumas*

The minute one utters a certainty, the opposite comes to mind.

— *May Sarton*

Human beings have an inalienable right to invent themselves.

— *Germaine Greer*

Life can only be understood backwards; but it must be lived forwards.

— *Soren Kierkegaard*

The past is a foreign country; they do things differently there.

— *L. P. Hartley*

To be able to look back upon one's past life with satisfaction is to live twice.

— *Lord Acton*

I look to the future because that's where I'm going to spend the rest of my life.

— *George Burns*

Never regret. If it's good, it's wonderful. If it's bad, it's experience.

— *Victoria Holt*

Live out of your imagination, not your history.

— *Stephen Covey*

You only live once—but if you work it right, once is enough.

—*Joe E. Lewis*

It's a poor sort of memory that only works backward.

— *Lewis Carroll*

When I discover who I am, I'll be free.

— *Ralph Ellison*

He will always be a slave who does not know how to live upon a little.

— *Horace*

A thousand words will not leave so deep an impression as one deed.

— *Henrik Ibsen*

That which does not kill us makes us stronger.

— *Friedrich Nietzsche*

Prudence and compromise are necessary means, but every man should have an impudent end which he will not compromise. — *Charles Horton Cooley*

It is not easy to find happiness in ourselves, and it is not possible to find it elsewhere. — *Agnes Repplier*

The grand essentials of happiness are: something to do, something to love, and something to hope for. — *Allan K. Chalmers*

Why do you have to be a nonconformist like everybody else? — *James Thurber*

The more refined one is, the more unhappy. — *Anton Chekhov*

Wisdom is the quality that keeps you from getting into situations where you need it. — *Doug Larson*

When I hear somebody sigh, "Life is hard," I am always tempted to ask, "Compared to what?" — *Sydney J. Harris*

The main things which seem to me important on their own account, and not merely as means to other things, are knowledge, art, instinctive happiness, and relations of friendship or affection. — *Bertrand Russell*

There are three constants in life ... change, choice and principles. — *Stephen Covey*

It's easier to go down a hill than up it but the view is much better at the top. — *Henry Ward Beecher*

Every exit is an entry somewhere.

— *Tom Stoppard*

Tradition is a guide and not a jailer.

— *W. Somerset Maugham*

Here is the test to find whether your mission on earth is finished: if you're alive, it isn't. — *Richard Bach*

Normal is nothing more than a cycle on a washing machine. — *Whoopi Goldberg*

Failure is unimportant. It takes courage to make a fool of yourself. — *Charlie Chaplin*

We are all special cases. — *Albert Camus*

We have been taught to believe that negative equals realistic and positive equals unrealistic. — *Susan Jeffers*

If egotism means a terrific interest in one's self, egotism is absolutely essential to efficient living. — *Arnold Bennett*

A person is only as good as what they love. — *Saul Bellow*

An inexhaustible good nature is one of the most precious gifts of heaven, spreading itself like oil over the troubled sea of thought, and keeping the mind smooth and equable in the roughest weather. — *Washington Irving*

A hunch is creativity trying to tell you something. — *Frank Capra*

The trouble with so many of us is that we underestimate the power of simplicity. We have a tendency, it seems, to over-complicate our lives and forget what's important and what's not. We tend to mistake movement for achievement. We tend to focus on activities instead of results. And as the pace of life continues to race along in the outside world, we forget that we have the power to control our lives regardless of what's going on outside. — *Robert Stuberg*

Women who seek to be equal with men lack ambition. — *Timothy Leary*

Science is organized knowledge. Wisdom is organized life.

— *Immanuel Kant*

Peace is when time doesn't matter as it passes by.

— *Maria Scholl*

Any philosophy that can be put in a nutshell belongs there.

— *Sydney J. Harris*

Where is here?

— *Northrop Frye*

Choosing Your Path

He who laughs, lasts!

— *Mary Pettibone Poole*

I live to laugh, and I laugh to live.

— *Milton Berle*

Enjoy life. There's plenty of time to be dead.

— *Hans Christian Andersen*

Live as though it were your last day on earth. Someday you will be right.

— *Robert Anthony*

Time is the coin of your life. It is the only coin you have, and only you can determine how it will be spent. Be careful lest you let other people spend it for you.

— *Carl Sandburg*

Suspect each moment, for it is a thief, tiptoeing away with more than it brings.

— *John Updike*

Regret for the things we did can be tempered by time; it is regret for the things we did not do that is inconsolable.

— *Sydney J. Harris*

Avoiding the phrase "I don't have time" will soon help you to realize that you do have the time needed for just about anything you choose to accomplish in life.   — *Bo Bennett*

Life is without meaning. You bring the meaning to it. The meaning of life is whatever you ascribe it to be. Being alive is the meaning.   — *Joseph Campbell*

If I had to live my life again, I'd make the same mistakes, only sooner.   — *Tallulah Bankhead*

It takes little talent to see what lies under one's nose, a good deal to know in what direction to point that organ.

— *W. H. Auden*

Some men see things as they are and ask, "Why?" I dream things that never were and ask, "Why not?"

— *Robert F. Kennedy*

Life loves to be taken by the lapel and told, "I'm with you, kid. Let's go."   — *Maya Angelou*

You've got to keep fighting—you've got to risk your life every six months to stay alive.   — *Elia Kazan*

A wise man will make more opportunities than he finds.

— *Francis Bacon*

Stop acting as if life is a rehearsal. Live this day as if it were your last. The past is over and gone. The future is not guaranteed.   — *Wayne Dyer*

Live as if you were living a second time, and as though you had acted wrongly the first time.   — *Viktor E. Frankl*

THE HUMAN SPIRIT

Love the moment, and the energy of that moment will spread beyond all boundaries.
— *Corita Kent*

If we take care of the moments, the years will take care of themselves.
— *Maria Edgeworth*

Life lived for tomorrow will always be just a day away from being realized.
— *Leo Buscaglia*

I have found that if you love life, life will love you back.
— *Arthur Rubinstein*

The words printed here are concepts. You must go through the experiences.
— *Saint Augustine*

Mix a little foolishness with your prudence: It's good to be silly at the right moment.
— *Horace*

Laugh at yourself first, before anyone else can.
— *Elsa Maxwell*

We could never learn to be brave and patient, if there were only joy in the world.
— *Helen Keller*

When you're through changing, you're through.
— *Bruce Barton*

Everyone thinks of changing the world, but no one thinks of changing himself.
— *Leo Tolstoy*

The third-rate mind is only happy when it is thinking with the majority. The second-rate mind is only happy when it is thinking with the minority. The first-rate mind is only happy when it is thinking.
— *A. A. Milne*

You are today where your thoughts have brought you; you will be tomorrow where your thoughts take you.
— *James Lane Allen*

There are things I can't force. I must adjust. There are times when the greatest change needed is a change of my viewpoint.

— *Denis Diderot*

Courage is saying, "Maybe what I'm doing isn't working; maybe I should try something else."

— *Anna Lappe*

He who loses wealth loses much; he who loses a friend loses more; but he that loses his courage loses all.

— *Miguel de Cervantes*

A life spent making mistakes is not only more honorable but more useful than a life spent in doing nothing.

— *George Bernard Shaw*

Eliminate something superfluous from your life. Break a habit. Do something that makes you feel insecure.

— *Piero Ferrucci*

The great pleasure in life is doing what people say you cannot do.

— *Walter Bagehot*

Even though you may want to move forward in your life, you may have one foot on the brakes. In order to be free, we must learn how to let go. Release the hurt. Release the fear. Refuse to entertain your old pain. The energy it takes to hang onto the past is holding you back from a new life. What is it you would let go of today?

— *Mary Manin Morrissey*

You've got to make a conscious choice every day to shed the old—whatever *the old* means for you.

— *Sarah Ban Breathnach*

Without change, something sleeps inside us, and seldom awakens. The sleeper must awaken.

— *Frank Herbert*

Change your thoughts and you change your world.

— *Norman Vincent Peale*

I would rather regret the things that I have done than the things that I have not.   — *Lucille Ball*

Never feel self-pity, the most destructive emotion there is. How awful to be caught up in the terrible squirrel cage of self
                                                    — *Millicent Fenwick*

One of the most adventurous things left us is to go to bed. For no one can lay a hand on our dreams.   — *E. V. Lucas*

Life is a great big canvas. Throw all the paint you can at it.
                                                    — *Danny Kaye*

The most pathetic person in the world is someone who has sight, but has no vision.   — *Helen Keller*

Use your imagination not to scare yourself to death but to inspire yourself to life.   — *Adele Brookman*

There's only one corner of the universe you can be certain of improving, and that's your own self.   — *Aldous Huxley*

The thing that is really hard, and really amazing, is giving up on being perfect and beginning the work of becoming yourself.   — *Anna Quindlen*

The easiest thing to be in the world is you. The most difficult thing to be is what other people want you to be. Don't let them put you in that position.   — *Leo Buscaglia*

To try to be better is to be better.
                                                    — *Charlotte Cushman*

The creative is the place where no one else has ever been. You have to leave the city of your comfort and go into the wilderness of your intuition. What you'll discover will be wonderful. What you'll discover will be yourself.   — *Alan Alda*

There are lots of ways of being miserable, but there's only one way of being comfortable, and that is to stop running round after happiness. If you make up your mind not to be happy there's no reason why you shouldn't have a fairly good time.

— EDITH WHARTON

Follow the grain in your own wood.

— *Howard Thurman*

In business or in life, don't follow the wagon tracks too closely.

— *H. Jackson Brown, Jr.*

Read, every day, something no one else is reading. Think, every day, something no one else is thinking. Do, every day, something no one else would be silly enough to do. It is bad for the mind to be always part of unanimity.

— *Christopher Morley*

The main thing is to keep the main thing the main thing.

— *Stephen Covey*

I still find each day too short for all the thoughts I want to think, all the walks I want to take, all the books I want to read, and all the friends I want to see. — *John Burroughs*

Think like a man of action, act like a man of thought.

— *Henri Bergson*

The smart ones ask when they don't know. And, sometimes when they do. — *Malcolm Forbes*

Trust yourself. Think for yourself. Act for yourself. Speak for yourself. Be yourself. Imitation is suicide. — *Marva Collins*

How can you come to know yourself? Never by thinking, always by doing. Try to do your duty, and you'll know right away what you amount to. —*Johann von Goethe*

All I want is a little more than I'll ever get.

— *Ashleigh Brilliant*

My candle burns at both ends
It will not last the night;
But ah, my foes, and oh, my friends—
It gives a lovely light.

— *Edna St. Vincent Millay*

The master in the art of living makes little distinction between his work and his play, his labor and his leisure, his mind and his body, his information and his recreation, his love and his religion. He hardly knows which is which. He simply pursues his vision of excellence at whatever he does, leaving others to decide whether he is working or playing. To him he's always doing both.

—*James A. Michener*

A smile is a curve that sets everything straight.

— *Phyllis Diller*

Act the way you'd like to be and soon you'll be the way you act.

— *Leonard Cohen*

Sometimes when I consider what tremendous consequences come from little things, I am tempted to think there are no little things. — *Bruce Barton*

Pick battles big enough to matter, small enough to win.

—*Jonathan Kozol*

To pretend, I actually do the thing: I have therefore only pretended to pretend. —*Jacques Derrida*

I define comfort as self-acceptance. When we finally learn that self-care begins and ends with ourselves, we no longer demand sustenance and happiness from others.

— *Jennifer Louden*

Happiness is different from pleasure. Happiness has something to do with struggling and enduring and accomplishing.

— *George Sheehan*

Happiness is neither virtue nor pleasure nor this thing nor that but simply growth. We are happy when we are growing.

— *William Butler Yeats*

No one is in control of your happiness but you; therefore, you have the power to change anything about yourself or your life that you want to change. — *Barbara De Angelis*

The Constitution only gives people the right to pursue happiness. You have to catch it yourself.

— *Benjamin Franklin*

It is the paradox of life that the way to miss pleasure is to seek it first. The very first condition of lasting happiness is that a life should be full of purpose, aiming at something outside self. — *Hugo Black*

You must try to generate happiness within yourself. If you aren't happy in one place, chances are you won't be happy anyplace. — *Ernie Banks*

Nobody really cares if you're miserable, so you might as well be happy. — *Cynthia Nelms*

It's a helluva start, being able to recognize what makes you happy. — *Lucille Ball*

I have no money, no resources, no hopes. I am the happiest man alive. — *Henry Miller*

THE HUMAN SPIRIT

Our subconscious minds have no sense of humor, play no jokes and cannot tell the difference between reality and an imagined thought or image. What we continually think about eventually will manifest in our lives. — *Robert Collier*

The art of being wise is the art of knowing what to overlook.
— *William James*

The remarkable thing is we have a choice every day regarding the attitude we will embrace for that day. We cannot change our past . . . we cannot change the fact that people will act in a certain way. We cannot change the inevitable. The only thing we can do is play on the one string we have, and that is our attitude. . . . I am convinced that life is 10 percent what happens to me and 90 percent how I react to it. And so it is with you. . . . We are in charge of our attitudes.
— *Charles Swindoll*

A positive attitude may not solve all your problems, but it will annoy enough people to make it worth the effort.
— *Herm Albright*

A proverb is no proverb to you till life has illustrated it.
—*John Keats*

When one man, for whatever reason, has the opportunity to lead an extraordinary life, he has no right to keep it to himself.
— *Jacques Yves Cousteau*

You desire to know the art of living, my friend? It is contained in one phrase: Make use of suffering.
— *Henri-Frédéric Amiel*

The truth that many people never understand, until it is too late, is that the more you try to avoid suffering the more you suffer because smaller and more insignificant things begin to torture you in proportion to your fear of being hurt.
— *Thomas Merton*

Don't judge each day by the harvest you reap but by the
seeds that you plant.   — *Robert Louis Stevenson*

Our lives improve only when we take chances—and the first
and most difficult risk we can take is to be honest with ourselves.   — *Walter Anderson*

Go confidently in the direction of your dreams! Live the life
you've imagined. As you simplify your life, the laws of the
universe will be simpler.   — *Henry David Thoreau*

An adventure is only an inconvenience rightly considered.
An inconvenience is only an adventure wrongly considered.
                                    — *G. K. Chesterton*

As a well-spent day brings happy sleep, so a life well spent
brings happy death.   — *Leonardo da Vinci*

Things turn out best for the people who make the best of
the way things turn out.   — *Art Linkletter*

If you can't get rid of the skeleton in your closet, you'd best
teach it to dance.   — *George Bernard Shaw*

The minute you settle for less than you deserve, you get even
less than you settled for.   — *Maureen Dowd*

To avoid criticism, do nothing, say nothing, and be nothing.
                                    — *Elbert Hubbard*

Blessed is he who expects nothing, for he shall never be
disappointed.   — *Alexander Pope*

I don't want to get to the end of my life and find that I lived
just the length of it. I want to have lived the width of it as well.
                                    — *Diane Ackerman*

The tragedy of life is not that it ends so soon, but that we
wait so long to begin it.   — *W. M. Lewis*

Doing your best at this moment puts you in the best place for the next moment.
— *Oprah Winfrey*

A woman who is convinced that she deserves to accept only the best challenges herself to give the best. Then she is living phenomenally.
— *Maya Angelou*

One of the keys to happiness is a bad memory.
— *Rita Mae Brown*

A pessimist is one who makes difficulties of his opportunities and an optimist is one who makes opportunities of his difficulties.
— *Harry S. Truman*

I am an optimist. It does not seem too much use being anything else.
— *Winston Churchill*

Stick with the optimists. It's going to be tough enough even if they're right.
— *James Reston*

Hope is the thing with feathers that perches in the soul.
— *Emily Dickinson*

Every tomorrow has two handles. We can take hold of it with the handle of anxiety or the handle of faith.
— *Henry Ward Beecher*

If you see ten troubles coming down the road, you can be sure that nine will run into the ditch before they reach you.
— *Calvin Coolidge*

We are confronted with insurmountable opportunities.
— *Walt Kelly*

No pessimist ever discovered the secret of the stars, or sailed to an uncharted land, or opened a new doorway for the human spirit.
— *Helen Keller*

Hitch your wagon to a star.

— *Ralph Waldo Emerson*

Aim at the sun, and you may not reach it; but your arrow will fly far higher than if aimed at an object on a level with yourself.

— *Joel Hawes*

The optimist proclaims that we live in the best of all possible worlds; and the pessimist fears this is true.

— *James Branch Cabell*

Sometimes people call me an idealist. Well, that is the way I know I am an American. America is the only idealistic nation in the world.

— *Woodrow Wilson*

Never leave that till tomorrow which you can do today.

— *Benjamin Franklin*

Never do today what you can put off till tomorrow. Delay may give clearer light as to what is best to be done.

— *Aaron Burr*

Remember, today is the tomorrow you worried about yesterday.

— *Dale Carnegie*

Forever is composed of nows.

— *Emily Dickinson*

Learning to ignore things is one of the great paths to inner peace.

— *Robert J. Sawyer*

Courage is the art of being the only one who knows you're scared to death.

— *Harold Wilson*

Courage is doing what you're afraid to do. There can be no courage unless you're scared.

— *Eddie Rickenbacker*

Whatever you do will be insignificant, but it is very important that you do it.

— *Mahatma Gandhi*

THE HUMAN SPIRIT

The greatest glory in living lies not in never falling, but in rising every time we fall. — *Nelson Mandela*

Blessed are they who heal you of self-despisings. Of all services which can be done to man, I know of none more precious. — *William Hale White*

The true test of character is not how much we know how to do, but how we behave when we don't know what to do. — *John Holt*

Experience is not what happens to a man. It is what a man does with what happens to him. — *Aldous Huxley*

What you do speaks so loud that I cannot hear what you say. — *Ralph Waldo Emerson*

Experience is that marvelous thing that enables you to recognize a mistake when you make it again. — *Franklin P. Jones*

Every action of our lives touches on some chord that will vibrate in eternity. — *Sean O'Casey*

Action is eloquence. — *William Shakespeare*

Mere brave speech without action is letting off useless steam. — *Mahatma Gandhi*

Knowledge is of no value unless you put it into practice. — *Anton Chekhov*

The man who insists on seeing with perfect clearness before he decides, never decides. — *Henri-Frédéric Amiel*

Surely there comes a time when counting the cost and paying the price aren't things to think about anymore. All that matters is value—the ultimate value of what one does. — *James Hilton*

He who joyfully marches in rank and file has already earned my contempt. He has been given a large brain by mistake, since for him the spinal cord would suffice.

— *Albert Einstein*

I must create a system, or be enslaved by another man's.

— *William Blake*

I have a simple philosophy. Fill what's empty. Empty what's full. And scratch where it itches.   — *Alice Roosevelt Longworth*

A strong positive mental attitude will create more miracles than any wonder drug.

— *Patricia Neal*

Look to your health; and if you have it, praise God and value it next to conscience; for health is the second blessing that we mortals are capable of, a blessing money can't buy.

— *Izaak Walton*

The human body experiences a powerful gravitational pull in the direction of hope. That is why the patient's hopes are the physician's secret weapon. They are the hidden ingredients in any prescription.   — *Norman Cousins*

When you can't remember why you're hurt, that's when you're healed.

— *Jane Fonda*

All sanity depends on this: that it should be a delight to feel heat strike the skin, a delight to stand upright, knowing the bones are moving easily under the flesh.

— *Doris Lessing*

How poor are they who have not patience! What wound did ever heal but by degrees?

— *William Shakespeare*

Water, air, and cleanness are the chief articles in my pharmacy.

— *Napoleon Bonaparte*

My doctor is wonderful. Once, in 1955, when I couldn't afford an operation, he touched up the X-rays.   *— Joey Bishop*

I think that age as a number is not nearly as important as health. You can be in poor health and be pretty miserable at 40 or 50. If you're in good health, you can enjoy things into your 80s.   *— Bob Barker*

Your heaviest artillery will be your will to live. Keep that big gun going.   *— Norman Cousins*

iving

I don't think there's any richer reward in life than helping someone. You can't measure it in money or fame or anything else. But if we're not put here for anything else but to help each other get through life, I think that's a very honorable existence.   *— Tom Brokaw*

What we have done for ourselves alone dies with us; what we have done for others and the world remains and is immortal.   *— Albert Pike*

In charity there is no excess.   *— Francis Bacon*

After the verb "to love," "to help" is the most beautiful verb in the world.   *— Bertha von Suttner*

Givers have to set limits because takers rarely do.

— Irma Kurtz

William Shakespeare

The World Is His Stage

For William Shakespeare, yes, the play was the thing.

Shakespeare was born in Stratford-on-Avon in 1564. He was not overly educated—his formal schooling ended at age 15. He plunged into London's theater scene as an actor and writer in the late 1580s, and by 1611 he had written the most highly regarded collection of plays in history. While one critic skewered Shakespeare as "an upstart crow," he was a great success in his own time—writing for London's foremost acting troupe and having his works published as popular literature.

While plenty is known about the structure of Shakespeare's life—his works, where he lived, and such—little is known about the man as a person.

Shakespeare had a heroic command of the language. Our modern tongue is lavishly dappled with words and phrases that are traced directly back to the Bard's pen, including, "To be or not to be—that is the question," "Out, damned spot!," "All the world's a stage," "Friends, Romans, countrymen," "Beware the ides of March," and "Something is rotten in the state of Denmark."

The first thing we do, let's kill all the lawyers.

The play's the thing
Wherein I'll catch the conscience of the king.

All the world's a stage,
And all the men and women merely players.
They have their exits and their entrances;
And one man in his time plays many parts.

Brevity is the soul of wit.

What a piece of work is man!

Cowards die many times before their deaths;
The valiant never taste of death but once.
Of all the wonders that I yet have heard,
It seems to me most strange that men should fear;
Seeing that death, a necessary end,
Will come when it will come.

Neither a borrower nor a lender be.

What's in a name? That which we call a rose
By any other name would smell as sweet.

Out, out, brief candle!
Life's but a walking shadow, a poor player
That struts and frets his hour upon the stage
And then is heard no more; it is a tale
Told by an idiot, full of sound and fury,
Signifying nothing.

The service we render to others is really the rent we pay for our room on this earth.

— *Wilfred Grenfell*

If you want others to be happy, practice compassion. If you want to be happy, practice compassion. — *The Dalai Lama*

Never look down on anybody unless you're helping him up.

—*Jesse Jackson*

Those who bring sunshine into the lives of others cannot keep it from themselves. — *James M. Barrie*

How wonderful it is that nobody need wait a single moment before starting to improve the world. — *Anne Frank*

You must give some time to your fellow men. Even if it's a little thing, do something for others—something for which you get no pay but the privilege of doing it.

— *Albert Schweitzer*

From what we get, we can make a living; what we give, however, makes a life. — *Arthur Ashe*

It's easy to make a buck. It's a lot tougher to make a difference.

— *Tom Brokaw*

The smallest deed is better than the greatest intention.

—*John Burroughs*

If I can stop one heart from breaking, I shall not live in vain.

— *Emily Dickinson*

A friend is a second self.

— ARISTOTLE

Relationships

At the end of your life, you will never regret not having passed one more test, not winning one more verdict or not closing one more deal. You will regret time not spent with a husband, a friend, a child, or a parent.
— *Barbara Bush*

The meeting of two personalities is like the contact of two chemical substances: if there is any reaction, both are transformed.
— *Carl Jung*

The true measure of a man is how he treats someone who can do him absolutely no good.
— *Ann Landers*

Isn't everyone a part of everyone else?
— *Budd Schulberg*

Good humor is one of the best articles of dress one can wear in society.
— *William Makepeace Thackeray*

Don't criticize what you don't understand, son. You never walked in that man's shoes.
— *Elvis Presley*

Until you walk a mile in another man's moccasins you can't imagine the smell.
— *Robert Byrne*

If a man be gracious and courteous to strangers, it shows he is a citizen of the world, and that his heart is no island cut off from other lands, but a continent that joins to them.
— *Francis Bacon*

The best time to make friends is before you need them.
— *Ethel Barrymore*

Friendship is the hardest thing in the world to explain. It's not something you learn in school. But if you haven't learned the meaning of friendship, you really haven't learned anything.

— *Muhammad Ali*

If you find it in your heart to care for somebody else, you will have succeeded.

— *Maya Angelou*

A true friend knows your weaknesses but shows you your strengths; feels your fears but fortifies your faith; sees your anxieties but frees your spirit; recognizes your disabilities but emphasizes your possibilities.

— *William Arthur Ward*

It is one of the blessings of old friends that you can afford to be stupid with them.

— *Ralph Waldo Emerson*

When you find the right people, you never let go. The people who count are the ones who are your friends in lean times. You have all the friends you want when things are going well.

— *James Lee Burke*

Every man should keep a fair-sized cemetery in which to bury the faults of his friends.

— *Henry Ward Beecher*

Treat your friends as you do your pictures, and place them in their best light.

— *Jennie Jerome Churchill*

Remember that the most valuable antiques are dear old friends.

— *H. Jackson Brown, Jr.*

The real test of friendship is: can you literally do nothing with the other person? Can you enjoy those moments of life that are utterly simple?

— *Eugene Kennedy*

Until you've lost your reputation, you never realize what a burden it was.

— *Margaret Mitchell*

THE HUMAN SPIRIT

One thing you will probably remember well is any time you forgive and forget.

— *Franklin P. Jones*

Whenever anyone has offended me, I try to raise my soul so high that the offense cannot reach it.

— *René Descartes*

Forgiveness is a virtue of the brave.

— *Indira Gandhi*

Life appears to me too short to be spent in nursing animosity or registering wrongs.

— *Charlotte Brontë*

Forget injuries; never forget kindnesses.

— *Confucius*

Forgiveness does not change the past, but it does enlarge the future.

— *Paul Boese*

You cannot go around and keep score. If you keep score on the good things and the bad things, you'll find out that you're a very miserable person. God gave man the ability to forget, which is one of the greatest attributes you have. Because if you remember everything that's happened to you, you generally remember that which is the most unfortunate.

— *Hubert H. Humphrey*

Holding on to anger, resentment and hurt only gives you tense muscles, a headache and a sore jaw from clenching your teeth. Forgiveness gives you back the laughter and the lightness in your life.

— *Joan Lunden*

Contrary to general belief, I do not believe that friends are necessarily the people you like best, they are merely the people who got there first.

— *Peter Ustinov*

I always like to know everything about my new friends, and nothing about my old ones.

— *Oscar Wilde*

If we listened to our intellect, we'd never have a love affair. We'd never have a friendship. We'd never go into business, because we'd be cynical. Well, that's nonsense. You've got to jump off cliffs all the time and build your wings on the way down.

— *Ray Bradbury*

You can make more friends in two months by becoming interested in other people than you can in two years by trying to get other people interested in you.

— *Dale Carnegie*

An ounce of loyalty is worth a pound of cleverness.

— *Elbert Hubbard*

When a friend is in trouble, don't annoy him by asking if there is anything you can do. Think up something appropriate and do it.

— *Edgar Watson Howe*

The real art of conversation is not only to say the right thing at the right place but to leave unsaid the wrong thing at the tempting moment.

— *Dorothy Nevill*

They may forget what you said, but they will never forget how you made them feel.

— *Carl W. Buechner*

Sometimes being a friend means mastering the art of timing. There is a time for silence. A time to let go.... And a time to prepare to pick up the pieces when it's all over.

— *Gloria Naylor*

If you're afraid to let someone else see your weakness, take heart: Nobody's perfect. Besides, your attempts to hide your flaws don't work as well as you think they do.

— *Julie Morgenstern*

Never apologize for showing feeling. When you do so, you apologize for the truth.

— *Benjamin Disraeli*

THE HUMAN SPIRIT

Laugh and the world laughs with you,
snore and you sleep alone.

— ANTHONY BURGESS

The joy that isn't shared dies young.

— *Anne Sexton*

Better to remain silent and be thought a fool than to speak
out and remove all doubt. — *Abraham Lincoln*

The most important thing in communication is to hear what
isn't being said. — *Peter F. Drucker*

Never miss a chance to keep your mouth shut.

— *Robert Newton Peck*

Be a good listener. Your ears will never get you in trouble.

— *Frank Tyger*

When people talk, listen completely. Most people never listen.

— *Ernest Hemingway*

The habit of common and continuous speech is a symptom
of mental deficiency. — *Walter Bagehot*

Men of few words are the best men.

— *William Shakespeare*

I have never been hurt by anything I didn't say.

— *Calvin Coolidge*

Don't talk unless you can improve the silence.

— *Jorge Luis Borges*

It's good to shut up sometimes.

— *Marcel Marceau*

No one has a finer command of language than the person who keeps his mouth shut. — *Sam Rayburn*

Lord, give us the wisdom to utter words that are gentle and tender, for tomorrow we may have to eat them.
— *Morris K. Udall*

A loud voice cannot compete with a clear voice, even if it's a whisper. — *Barry Neil Kaufman*

One voice can enter ten ears, but ten voices cannot enter one ear. — *Leone Levi*

We have two ears and one tongue so that we would listen more and talk less. — *Diogenes*

When you talk, you repeat what you already know; when you listen, you often learn something. — *Jared Sparks*

When you say yes, say it quickly. But always take a half hour to say no, so you can understand the other fellow's side.
— *Francis Cardinal Spellman*

The only reward of virtue is virtue; the only way to have a friend is to be one. — *Ralph Waldo Emerson*

No man has the right to dictate what other men should perceive, create or produce, but all should be encouraged to reveal themselves, their perceptions and emotions, and to build confidence in the creative spirit. — *Ansel Adams*

Seek first to understand, then to be understood.
— *Stephen Covey*

A slip of the foot you may soon recover, but a slip of the tongue you may never get over. — *Benjamin Franklin*

People will accept your ideas much more readily if you tell them Benjamin Franklin said it first. — *David H. Comins*

Everything that irritates us about others can lead us to an understanding of ourselves.

— Carl Jung

You can tell whether a man is clever by his answers. You can tell whether a man is wise by his questions.

— Naguib Mahfouz

Just when you think that a person is just a backdrop for the rest of the universe, watch them and see that they laugh, they cry, they tell jokes . . . they're just friends waiting to be made.

— Jeffrey Borenstein

A chief event of life is the day in which we have encountered a mind that startled us.

— Ralph Waldo Emerson

We are here on earth to do good to others. What the others are here for, I don't know.

— W. H. Auden

Good manners will open doors that the best education cannot.

— Clarence Thomas

Personality can open doors, but only character can keep them open.

— Elmer G. Letterman

Our character is what we do when we think no one is looking.

— H. Jackson Brown, Jr.

Public behavior is merely private character writ large.

— Stephen Covey

Don't reserve your best behavior for special occasions. You can't have two sets of manners, two social codes—one for those you admire and want to impress, another for those whom you consider unimportant. You must be the same to all people.

— Lillian Eichler Watson

Politeness and consideration for others is like investing pennies and getting dollars back.

— Thomas Sowell

The true secret of giving advice is, after you have honestly given it, to be perfectly indifferent whether it is taken or not, and never persist in trying to set people right.

— *Hannah Whitall Smith*

Tact is the knack of making a point without making an enemy.

— *Isaac Newton*

I believe in an open mind, but not so open that your brains fall out.

— *Arthur Hays Sulzberger*

I love to be alone. I never found the companion that was so companionable as solitude.

— *Henry David Thoreau*

No man is an island, entire of itself; every man is a piece of the continent.

— *John Donne*

Living apart and at peace with myself, I came to realize more vividly the meaning of the doctrine of acceptance. To refrain from giving advice, to refrain from meddling in the affairs of others, to refrain, even though the motives be the highest, from tampering with another's way of life—so simple, yet so difficult for an active spirit. Hands off!

— *Henry Miller*

If your happiness depends on what somebody else does, I guess you do have a problem.

— *Richard Bach*

As experience widens, one begins to see how much upon a level all human things are.

— *Joseph Farrell*

As I grow older, I pay less attention to what men say. I just watch what they do.

— *Andrew Carnegie*

I have witnessed the softening of the hardest of hearts by a simple smile.

— GOLDIE HAWN

THE HUMAN SPIRIT

Tears shed for self are tears of weakness, but tears shed for others are a sign of strength. — *Billy Graham*

Minds are like parachutes; they work best when open.
— *Thomas Dewar*

Too often we underestimate the power of a touch, a smile, a kind word, a listening ear, an honest compliment, or the smallest act of caring, all of which have the potential to turn a life around. — *Leo Buscaglia*

The bird a nest, the spider a web, man friendship.
— *William Blake*

To be successful you have to be selfish, or else you never achieve. And once you get to your highest level, then you have to be unselfish. Stay reachable. Stay in touch. Don't isolate. — *Michael Jordan*

I am not in this world to live up to other people's expectations, nor do I feel that the world must live up to mine.
— *Fritz Perls*

We judge ourselves by what we feel capable of doing, while others judge us by what we have already done.
— *Henry Wadsworth Longfellow*

Beginning today, treat everyone you meet as if they were going to be dead by midnight. Extend them all the care, kindness and understanding you can muster. Your life will never be the same again. — *Og Mandino*

It is not rejection itself that people fear, it is the possible consequences of rejection. Preparing to accept those consequences and viewing rejection as a learning experience that will bring you closer to success, will not only help you to conquer the fear of rejection, but help you to appreciate rejection itself.
— *Bo Bennett*

*L*ao-tzu

Wisdom of the Ages

According to legend, Lao-tzu was curator of the Chinese imperial archives in the 6th century B.C.

Steeped in such a wealth of history and philosophy, Lao-tzu became a wise man himself. Upon retiring, he left civilization. As he passed through a gate in the Great Wall, a border guard asked him to record what he had learned for posterity. Lao-tzu complied and authored a small book of concise and profound thoughts. These writings, now called the *Tao Te Ching,* advocate a passive, intuitive way of behavior—living in harmony with a cosmic unity that underlies everything.

While Lao-tzu is credited with being the founder of Taoism and one of the best-known of the Chinese philosophers, scholars disagree as to whether he actually existed. Some theorize that his writings are a collection of teachings from a number of sources.

*

A journey of a thousand miles begins with a single step.

*

He who knows others is wise; he who knows himself is enlightened.

*

To have little is to possess. To have plenty is to be perplexed.

*

In the world there is nothing more submissive and weak than water. Yet for attacking that which is hard and strong nothing can surpass it.

*

A good traveler has no fixed plans, and is not intent on arriving.

*

*To realize that you do not understand is a virtue;
not to realize that you do not understand is a defect.*

*

*A leader is best when people barely know he exists.
When his work is done, his aim fulfilled, they will say,
"We did it ourselves."*

The best way to cheer yourself up is to try to cheer somebody
else up.   — *Mark Twain*

If you have only one smile in you, give it to the people you
love. Don't be surly at home, then go out in the street and
start grinning "Good morning" at total strangers.
                                                       — *Maya Angelou*

Ask yourself: Have you been kind today? Make kindness your
daily modus operandi and change your world.
                                                       — *Annie Lennox*

We cannot hold a torch to light another's path without
brightening our own.   — *Ben Sweetland*

All of us, at certain moments of our lives, need to take advice
and to receive help from other people.   — *Alexis Carrel*

I was shy for several years in my early days in Hollywood
until I figured out that no one really gave a damn if I was
shy or not, and I got over my shyness.   — *Lucille Ball*

It is far more impressive when others discover your good
qualities without your help.   — *Judith Martin*

Always hold your head up, but be careful to keep your nose
at a friendly level.   — *Max L. Forman*

One must have a good memory to be able to keep the prom-
ises one makes.   — *Friedrich Nietzsche*

People with courage and character always seem sinister to
the rest.   — *Hermann Hesse*

I hope that people will finally come to realize that there is
only one "race"—the human race—and that we are all mem-
bers of it.   — *Margaret Atwood*

THE HUMAN SPIRIT

People are unreasonable, illogical, and self-centered. Love
them anyway.
— *Mother Teresa*

Chance and Destiny

Fortune knocks but once, but misfortune has much more
patience.
— *Laurence J. Peter*

Life consists not in holding good cards but in playing those
you hold well.
— *Josh Billings*

The cards are ill shuffled till I have a good hand.
— *Jonathan Swift*

Life is like a game of cards. The hand that is dealt you is
determinism; the way you play it is free will.
— *Jawaharlal Nehru*

In the field of observation, chance favors only the prepared
mind.
— *Louis Pasteur*

If you don't like something, change it. If you can't change it,
change your attitude. Don't complain.
— *Maya Angelou*

Make no little plans; they have no magic to stir men's
blood....Make big plans, aim high in hope and work.
— *Daniel H. Burnham*

Take a chance! All life is a chance. The man who goes
furthest is generally the one who is willing to do and dare.
— *Dale Carnegie*

Luck is what you have left over after you give 100 percent.
— *Langston Coleman*

Luck? I don't know anything about luck. I've never banked on it and I'm afraid of people who do. Luck to me is something else: Hard work—and realizing what is opportunity and what isn't.
— *Lucille Ball*

Chance is always powerful. Let your hook be always cast; in the pool where you least expect it, there will be a fish.
— *Ovid*

The only sure thing about luck is that it will change.
— *Bret Harte*

True luck consists not in holding the best of the cards at the table; luckiest is he who knows just when to rise and go home.
— *John Hay*

Those who trust to chance must abide by the results of chance.
— *Calvin Coolidge*

We must believe in luck. For how else can we explain the success of those we don't like?
— *Jean Cocteau*

Luck is not something you can mention in the presence of self-made men.
— *E. B. White*

Success is simply a matter of luck. Ask any failure.
— *Earl Wilson*

We cannot direct the wind, but we can adjust the sails.
— *Bertha Calloway*

We need to learn to set our course by the stars, not by the light of every passing ship.
— *Omar N. Bradley*

I am not afraid of storms, for I am learning how to sail my ship.
— *Louisa May Alcott*

THE HUMAN SPIRIT

When one door of happiness closes, another opens; but often we look so long at the closed door that we do not see the one which has opened for us.

— HELEN KELLER

Even if you're on the right track, you'll get run over if you just sit there.

— *Will Rogers*

The Chinese use two brush strokes to write the word *crisis*. One brush stroke stands for danger; the other for opportunity. In a crisis, be aware of the danger—but recognize the opportunity.

— *Richard M. Nixon*

Do not count your chickens before they are hatched.

— *Aesop*

The grass is not, in fact, always greener on the other side of the fence. Fences have nothing to do with it. The grass is greenest where it is watered. When crossing over fences, carry water with you and tend the grass wherever you may be.

— *Robert Fulghum*

To look backward for a while is to refresh the eye, to restore it, and to render it the more fit for its prime function of looking forward.

— *Margaret Fairless Barber*

The doors we open and close each day decide the lives we live.

— *Flora Whittemore*

I have become my own version of an optimist. If I can't make it through one door, I'll go through another door—or I'll make a door. Something terrific will come no matter how dark the present.

— *Joan Rivers*

I don't want to be a passenger in my own life.
— *Diane Ackerman*

No trumpets sound when the important decisions of our life are made. Destiny is made known silently.   — *Agnes de Mille*

The important thing is this: to be able at any moment to sacrifice what we are for what we could become.
— *Charles Du Bos*

The past is a source of knowledge, and the future is a source of hope. Love of the past implies faith in the future.
— *Stephen Ambrose*

Destiny is not a matter of chance, it is a matter of choice; it is not a thing to be waited for, it is a thing to be achieved.
— *William Jennings Bryan*

If you don't run your own life, somebody else will.
— *John Atkinson*

If you can find a path with no obstacles, it probably doesn't lead anywhere.   — *Frank A. Clark*

The 50-50-90 rule: Anytime you have a 50-50 chance of getting something right, there's a 90 percent probability you'll get it wrong.   — *Andy Rooney*

We have to believe in free will. We've got no choice.
— *Isaac Bashevis Singer*

Of course the game is rigged. Don't let that stop you—if you don't play, you can't win.   — *Robert A. Heinlein*

In reality, serendipity accounts for one percent of the blessings we receive in life, work and love. The other 99 percent is due to our efforts.   — *Peter McWilliams*

Shallow men believe in luck. Strong men believe in cause and effect.

— *Ralph Waldo Emerson*

Our problems are man-made, therefore they may be solved by man. And man can be as big as he wants. No problem of human destiny is beyond human beings.

— *John F. Kennedy*

Two roads diverged in a wood,
and I—I took the one less traveled by,
And that has made all the difference.

— *Robert Frost*

If you want a guarantee, buy a toaster.

— *Clint Eastwood*

Hope for the best. Expect the worst.
Life is a play. We're unrehearsed.

— *Mel Brooks*

Expect the best. Prepare for the worst. Capitalize on what comes.

— *Zig Ziglar*

Nothing happens to anybody which he is not fitted by nature to bear.

— *Marcus Aurelius*

Ask many of us who are disabled what we would like in life and you would be surprised how few would say, "Not to be disabled." We accept our limitations.

— *Itzhak Perlman*

I have gained this by philosophy: that I do without being commanded what others do only from fear of the law.

— *Aristotle*

The price of greatness is responsibility.

— *Winston Churchill*

Success on any major scale requires you to accept responsibility....In the final analysis, the one quality that all successful people have...Is the ability to take on responsibility.

— *Michael Korda*

To be mature means to face, and not evade, every fresh crisis that comes.

— *Fritz Kunkel*

He who is slowest in making a promise is most faithful in its performance.

—*Jean-Jacques Rousseau*

I am free, no matter what rules surround me. If I find them tolerable, I tolerate them; if I find them too obnoxious, I break them. I am free because I know that I alone am morally responsible for everything I do.

— *Robert A. Heinlein*

You are remembered for the rules you break.

— *Douglas MacArthur*

Once a word has been allowed to escape, it cannot be recalled.

— *Horace*

It is thrifty to prepare today for the wants of tomorrow.

— *Aesop*

Men acquire a particular quality by constantly acting a particular way...You become just by performing just actions, temperate by performing temperate actions, brave by performing brave actions.

— *Aristotle*

The oldest, shortest words—"yes" and "no"—are those which require the most thought.

— *Pythagoras*

Do not wait for extraordinary circumstances to do good; try to use ordinary situations.

—*Jean Paul Richter*

THE HUMAN SPIRIT

Right and Wrong

Good judgment comes from experience, and experience comes from bad judgment. — *Barry LePatner*

Real integrity is doing the right thing, knowing that nobody's going to know whether you did it or not.
— *Oprah Winfrey*

My soul refuses to be satisfied so long as it is a helpless witness of a single wrong or a single misery. But it is not possible for me, a weak, frail, miserable being, to mend every wrong or to hold myself free of blame for all the wrong I see.
— *Mahatma Gandhi*

In matters of style, swim with the current; in matters of principle, stand like a rock. — *Thomas Jefferson*

Good sense about trivialities is better than nonsense about things that matter. — *Max Beerbohm*

The character of every act depends upon the circumstances in which it is done. — *Oliver Wendell Holmes, Jr.*

Do what you feel in your heart to be right—
for you'll be criticized anyway. You'll be
damned if you do, and damned if you don't.

— ELEANOR ROOSEVELT

You should examine yourself daily. If you find faults, you should correct them. When you find none, you should try even harder. — *Xi Zhi*

I would rather be the man who bought the Brooklyn Bridge than the man who sold it. — *Will Rogers*

I firmly believe that the Gandhian philosophy of nonviolent resistance is the only logical and moral approach to the solution of the race problem in the United States.
— *Martin Luther King, Jr.*

It is happier to be sometimes cheated than not to trust.
— *Samuel Johnson*

Common sense is the knack of seeing things as they are, and doing things as they ought to be done. — *Josh Billings*

The time is always right to do what is right.
— *Martin Luther King, Jr.*

A thought which does not result in an action is nothing much, and an action which does not proceed from a thought is nothing at all. — *Georges Bernanos*

To have a right to do a thing is not at all the same as to be right in doing it. — *G. K. Chesterton*

There can be no happiness if the things we believe in are different from the things we do. — *Freya Stark*

The only correct actions are those that demand no explanation and no apology. — *Red Auerbach*

Chase after truth like hell and you'll free yourself, even though you never touch its coat-tails. — *Clarence Darrow*

By the time a man realizes that maybe his father was right, he usually has a son who thinks he's wrong.

— *Charles Wadsworth*

There are few nudities so objectionable as the naked truth

— *Agnes Repplier*

When I tell the truth, it is not for the sake of convincing those who do not know it, but for the sake of defending those that do.

— *William Blake*

If there's any message to my work, it is ultimately that it's okay to be different, that it's good to be different, that we should question ourselves before we pass judgment on someone who looks different, behaves different, talks different, is a different color.

— *Johnny Depp*

Don't ever become a pessimist....A pessimist is correct oftener than an optimist, but an optimist has more fun, and neither can stop the march of events.

— *Robert A. Heinlein*

Never let your sense of morals prevent you from doing what's right.

— *Isaac Asimov*

Like an unchecked cancer, hate corrodes the personality and eats away its vital unity. Hate destroys a man's sense of values and his objectivity. It causes him to describe the beautiful as ugly and the ugly as beautiful, and to confuse the true with the false and the false with the true.

— MARTIN LUTHER KING, JR.

3

Modern Life

The musings on the following pages cover all of the topics that the caveman never contemplated—work life, computers, celebrity, money, and more. Indeed, some were unheard-of a mere half-century ago.

*W*ork

Genius is 1 percent inspiration, 99 percent perspiration.

— Thomas Alva Edison

Underpromise; overdeliver.

— Tom Peters

The key is not to prioritize what's on your schedule, but to schedule your priorities.

— Stephen Covey

Give me a stock clerk with a goal and I'll give you a man who will make history. Give me a man with no goals and I'll give you a stock clerk.

— J. C. Penney

Nothing is particularly hard if you divide it into small jobs.

— Henry Ford

The way to get started is to quit talking and begin doing.

— Walt Disney

Opportunity is missed by most people because it is dressed in overalls and looks like work.

— Thomas Alva Edison

Don't stay in bed, unless you can make money in bed.

— George Burns

It's a job that's never started that takes the longest to finish.

—J.R.R. Tolkien

The only place where success comes before work is in a dictionary.

— Vidal Sassoon

The more I want to get something done, the less I call it work.

— Richard Bach

MODERN LIFE

Choose a job you love, and you will never have to work a day in your life.
— *Confucius*

The ability to focus attention on important things is a defining characteristic of intelligence
— *Robert J. Shiller*

Being on a tightrope is living; everything else is waiting.
— *Karl Wallenda*

One thing life has taught me: If you are interested, you never have to look for new interests. They come to you. When you are genuinely interested in one thing, it will always lead to something else.
— *Eleanor Roosevelt*

I believe you are your work. Don't trade the stuff of your life, time, for nothing more than dollars. That's a rotten bargain.
— *Rita Mae Brown*

Work joyfully and peacefully, knowing that right thoughts and right efforts inevitably bring about right results.
—*James Allen*

Anyone can dabble, but once you've made that commitment, your blood has that particular thing in it, and it's very hard for people to stop you.
— *Bill Cosby*

Find a job you like and you add five days to every week.
— *H. Jackson Brown, Jr.*

Work as if you were to live a hundred years,
Pray as if you were to die tomorrow.
— *Benjamin Franklin*

Some critics will write "Maya Angelou is a natural writer"— which is right after being a natural heart surgeon.
— *Maya Angelou*

What we really want to do is what we are really meant to do. When we do what we are meant to do, money comes to us, doors open for us, we feel useful, and the work we do feels like play to us. — *Julia Cameron*

The key is to figure out what you want out of life, not what you want out of your career. — *Goldie Hawn*

Nothing is really work unless you would rather be doing something else. — *James M. Barrie*

Never continue in a job you don't enjoy. If you're happy in what you're doing, you'll like yourself, you'll have inner peace. And if you have that, along with physical health, you will have had more success than you could possibly have imagined. — *Johnny Carson*

It's just a job. Grass grows, birds fly, waves pound the sand. I beat people up. — *Muhammad Ali*

A mule will labor 10 years willingly and patiently for you, for the privilege of kicking you once. — *William Faulkner*

I do not pray for a lighter load, but for a stronger back. — *Phillips Brooks*

Creative ideas flourish best in a shop which preserves some spirit of fun. Nobody is in business for fun, but that does not mean there cannot be fun in business. — *Leo Burnett*

Creativity is a drug I cannot live without. — *Cecil B. DeMille*

Creativity is allowing yourself to make mistakes. Art is knowing which ones to keep. — SCOTT ADAMS

Creativity represents a miraculous coming together of the uninhibited energy of the child with its apparent opposite and enemy, the sense of order imposed on the disciplined adult intelligence.
— *Norman Podhoretz*

There is only one admirable form of the imagination: the imagination that is so intense that it creates a new reality, that it makes things happen.
— *Sean O'Faolain*

Of all the useless things a person can do, limerick writing is right up there with golf and fishing.
— *Garrison Keillor*

Creativity comes from trust. Trust your instincts. And never hope more than you work.
— *Rita Mae Brown*

Keep on going and the chances are you will stumble on something, perhaps when you are least expecting it. I have never heard of anyone stumbling on something sitting down.
— *Charles F. Kettering*

You do things when the opportunities come along. I've had periods in my life when I've had a bundle of ideas come along, and I've had long dry spells. If I get an idea next week, I'll do something. If not, I won't do a damn thing.
— *Warren Buffett*

When inspiration does not come to me, I go halfway to meet it.
— *Sigmund Freud*

Creativity requires the courage to let go of certainties.
— *Erich Fromm*

Punishing honest mistakes stifles creativity. I want people moving and shaking the earth and they're going to make mistakes.
— *H. Ross Perot*

You live and learn. At any rate, you live.
— *Douglas Adams*

Be nice to people on your way up because you meet them on your way down.
— Jimmy Durante

If you haven't found something strange during the day, it hasn't been much of a day.
— John A. Wheeler

A dead end can never be a one-way street; you can always turn around and take another road.
— Bo Bennett

Those who do not want to imitate anything, produce nothing.
— Salvador Dalí

If we keep doing what we're doing, we're going to keep getting what we're getting.
— Stephen Covey

Don't worry about people stealing an idea. If it's original, you will have to ram it down their throats.
— Howard Aiken

Originality is unexplored territory. You get there by carrying a canoe—you can't take a taxi.
— Alan Alda

In order to be irreplaceable one must always be different.
— Coco Chanel

Dressing up is inevitably a substitute for good ideas. It is no coincidence that technically inept business types are known as "suits."
— Paul Graham

The secret to creativity is knowing how to hide your sources.
— Albert Einstein

Precision is not reality.
— Henri Matisse

Good questions outrank easy answers.
— Paul A. Samuelson

Quality questions create a quality life. Successful people ask better questions, and as a result, they get better answers.
— Tony Robbins

Creativity can solve almost any problem. The creative act, the defeat of habit by originality, overcomes everything.

— *George Lois*

It everyone says you are wrong, you're one step ahead. If everyone laughs at you, you're two steps ahead.

— *Charles "Chic" Thompson*

Curiosity about life in all of its aspects, I think, is still the secret of great creative people. — *Leo Burnett*

Intuition becomes increasingly valuable in the new information society precisely because there is so much data.

— *John Naisbitt*

Progress isn't made by early risers. It's made by lazy men trying to find easier ways to do something. — *Robert A. Heinlein*

You can't build a reputation on what you are going to do.

— *Henry Ford*

You've achieved success in your field when you don't know whether what you're doing is work or play. — *Warren Beatty*

Anyone can do any amount of work provided it isn't the work he is supposed to be doing at the moment.

— *Robert Benchley*

Slump, and the world slumps with you. Push, and you push alone. — *Laurence J. Peter*

Work is much more fun than fun. — *Noël Coward*

To be worn out is to be renewed. — *Lao-tzu*

Get happiness out of your work or you may never know what happiness is. — *Elbert Hubbard*

You have freedom when you're easy in your harness.

— *Robert Frost*

The harder you work, the luckier you get.

— *Gary Player*

Diamonds are nothing more than chunks of coal that stuck to their jobs.

— *Malcolm Forbes*

There seems to be some perverse human characteristic that likes to make easy things difficult.

— *Warren Buffett*

I've only been doing this 54 years. With a little experience, I might get better.

— *Harry Caray*

Whether you think you can or think you can't, you're right.

— *Henry Ford*

If I had eight hours to chop down a tree, I'd spend six hours sharpening my ax.

— *Abraham Lincoln*

I'm not a lawyer. I have many other faults but that is not one of them.

— *Ed Broadbent*

I've always believed that if you put in the work, the results will come. I don't do things half-heartedly. Because I know if I do, then I can expect half-hearted results.

— *Michael Jordan*

I don't wait for moods. You accomplish nothing if you do that. Your mind must know it has got to get down to work.

— *Pearl S. Buck*

The society which scorns excellence in plumbing as a humble activity and tolerates shoddiness in philosophy because it is an exalted activity will have neither good plumbing nor good philosophy: neither its pipes nor its theories will hold water.

— *John W. Gardner*

There is no labor a person does that is undignified—if they do it right.

— *Bill Cosby*

If a man is called to be a street sweeper, he should sweep streets even as Michelangelo painted, or Beethoven composed music, or Shakespeare wrote poetry. He should sweep streets so well that all the hosts of heaven and earth will pause to say, Here lived a great street sweeper who did his job well.

— *Martin Luther King, Jr.*

Don't rule out working with your hands. It does not preclude using your head.

— *Andy Rooney*

You can't fake quality any more than you can fake a good meal.

— *William S. Burroughs*

People forget how fast you did a job—but they remember how well you did it.

— *Howard Newton*

Tradition is what you resort to when you don't have the time or the money to do it right.

— *Kurt Herbert Alder*

Be true to your work, your word, and your friend.

— *Henry David Thoreau*

You'll never prove you're too good for a job by not doing your best.

— *Ethel Merman*

Labor disgraces no man; unfortunately, you occasionally find men who disgrace labor.

— *Ulysses S. Grant*

Only those who want everything done for them are bored.

— *Billy Graham*

You can't wait for inspiration. You have to go after it with a club.

— *Jack London*

Getting ahead in a difficult profession requires avid faith in yourself. That is why some people with mediocre talent, but with great inner drive, go much further than people with vastly superior talent.   — *Sophia Loren*

Formula for success: Rise early, work hard, strike oil.
                                                              — *J. Paul Getty*

These days, the mind that's standing still is, in fact, slipping backwards down the competitive ladder. Fast.   — *Tom Peters*

Careers, like rockets, don't always take off on time. The trick is to always keep the engine running.   — *Gary Sinise*

A good way I know to find happiness, is to not bore a hole to fit the plug.   — *Josh Billings*

Be miserable. Or motivate yourself. Whatever has to be done, it's always your choice.   — *Wayne Dyer*

Make every thought, every fact, that comes into your mind pay you a profit. Make it work and produce for you. Think of things not as they are but as they might be. Don't merely dream—but create!   — *Robert Collier*

A professional is someone who can do his best work when he doesn't feel like it.   — *Alistair Cooke*

It is necessary to work, if not from inclination, at least from despair. Everything considered, work is less boring than amusing oneself.   — *Charles Baudelaire*

The real man is one who always finds excuses for others, but never excuses himself.   — *Henry Ward Beecher*

Hard work spotlights the character of people: Some turn up their sleeves, some turn up their noses, and some don't turn up at all.   — *Sam Ewing*

In the modern world of business, it is useless to be a creative original thinker unless you can also sell what you create. Management cannot be expected to recognize a good idea unless it is presented to them by a good salesman.

— DAVID M. OGILVY

The time to repair the roof is when the sun is shining.
—John F. Kennedy

Work while you have the light. You are responsible for the talent that has been entrusted to you.
— Henri-Frédéric Amiel

From each according to his abilities, to each according to his needs.
— Louis Blanc

Do the hard jobs first. The easy jobs will take care of themselves.
— Dale Carnegie

Everything comes to him who hustles while he waits.
— Thomas Alva Edison

I'm impressed with the people from Chicago. Hollywood is hype, New York is talk, Chicago is work.
— Michael Douglas

Some people see things that are and ask, Why? Some people dream of things that never were and ask, Why not? Some people have to go to work and don't have time for all that.
— George Carlin

Appealing workplaces are to be avoided. One wants a room with no view, so imagination can meet memory in the dark.
— Annie Dillard

There is time for work. And time for love. That leaves no
other time.   — Coco Chanel

It has been my experience that one cannot, in any shape or
form, depend on human relations for lasting reward. It is only
work that truly satisfies.   — Bette Davis

Success is a journey, not a destination. The doing is often
more important than the outcome.   — Arthur Ashe

Enthusiasm is *not* the same as just being excited. One gets
excited about going on a roller coaster. One becomes enthu-
siastic about creating and building a roller coaster.
                                                    — Bo Bennett

Promise is the capacity for letting people down.
                                                 — Cyril Connolly

Try as hard as we may for perfection, the net result of our
labors is an amazing variety of imperfectness. We are surprised at our own versatility in being able to fail in so many
different ways.   — Samuel McChord Crothers

Being busy does not always mean real work. The object of all
work is production or accomplishment and to either of these
ends there must be forethought, system, planning, intelligence, and honest purpose, as well as perspiration. Seeming
to do is not doing.   — Thomas Alva Edison

Hell, there are no rules here—we're trying to accomplish
something.   — Thomas Alva Edison

Rules are made for people who aren't willing to make up
their own.   — Chuck Yeager

I work for him despite his faults and he lets me work for him
despite my deficiencies.   — Bill Moyers

Few great men would have got past personnel.

— *Paul Goodman*

My greatest strength as a consultant is to be ignorant and ask a few questions.   — *Peter F. Drucker*

How lucky Adam was. He knew when he said a good thing, nobody had said it before. Adam was not alone in the Garden of Eden, however, and does not deserve all the credit; much is due to Eve, the first woman, and Satan, the first consultant.

— *Mark Twain*

Consultants have credibility because they are not dumb enough to work at your company.   — *Scott Adams*

A desk is a dangerous place from which to watch the world.

— *John le Carré*

Nothing interferes with my concentration. You could put on an orgy in my office and I wouldn't look up. Well, maybe once.

— *Isaac Asimov*

Moving fast is not the same as going somewhere.

— *Robert Anthony*

If the only tool you have is a hammer, you tend to see every problem as a nail.   — *Abraham Maslow*

Farming looks mighty easy when your plow is a pencil, and you're a thousand miles from the corn field.

— *Dwight D. Eisenhower*

When we ask for advice, we are usually looking for an accomplice.   — *Saul Bellow*

It is easier to do a job right than to explain why you didn't.

— *Martin Van Buren*

Anything not worth doing is worth not doing well. Think about it.   — *Elias Schwartz*

I have not failed. I've just found 10,000 ways that won't work.
                                        — *Thomas Alva Edison*

A mistake is simply another way of doing things.
                                        — *Katharine Graham*

Experience is simply the name we give our mistakes.
                                        — *Oscar Wilde*

I have yet to see any problem, however complicated, which, when you looked at it in the right way, did not become still more complicated.   — *Paul Anderson*

The problem is not that there are problems. The problem is expecting otherwise and thinking that having problems is a problem.   — *Theodore Rubin*

The best way to escape from a problem is to solve it.
                                        — *Alan Saporta*

Each success only buys an admission ticket to a more difficult problem.   — *Henry Kissinger*

If you think your boss is stupid, remember: You wouldn't have a job if he was any smarter.   — *John Gotti*

Carpe per diem—seize the check.   — *Robin Williams*

The two most beautiful words in the English language are "check enclosed."   — *Dorothy Parker*

I like work: it fascinates me. I can sit and look at it for hours.
                                        — *Jerome K. Jerome*

Work expands so as to fill the time available for its completion.
                                        — *C. Northcote Parkinson*

I have long been of the opinion that if work were such a

splendid thing the rich would have kept more of it for themselves.   — *Bruce Grocott*

Men think highly of those who rise rapidly in the world; whereas nothing rises quicker than dust, straw, and feathers.
                                      — *Lord Byron*

I am a friend of the working man, and I would rather be his friend, than be one.   — *Clarence Darrow*

The only thing I was fit for was to be a writer, and this notion rested solely on my suspicion that I would never be fit for real work, and that writing didn't require any.
                                      — *Russell Baker*

Spare no expense to save money on this one.
                                      — *Samuel Goldwyn*

American business long ago gave up on demanding that prospective employees be honest and hardworking. It has even stopped hoping for employees who are educated enough that they can tell the difference between the men's room and the women's room without having little pictures on the doors.   — *Dave Barry*

A young man fills out an application for a job and does well until he gets to the last question, "Who should we notify in case of an accident?" He mulls it over and then writes, "Anybody in sight!"   — *Milton Berle*

Sometimes the best, and only effective, way to kill an idea is to put it into practice.   — *Sydney J. Harris*

I work until beer o'clock.   — *Stephen King*

All I've ever wanted was an honest week's pay for an honest day's work.
                                      — STEVE MARTIN

$\mathcal{B}$ureaucracy
Gone
Berserk

Sorry, dear readers, but you won't be allowed to read this particular collection of quotations on the subject of bureaucracy until you have presented three forms of photo ID and have filled out the application form in triplicate. Why? Because that's the way it's always been done.

In a hierarchy, every employee tends to rise to his level of incompetence.

— Laurence J. Peter

It's a poor bureaucrat who can't stall a good idea until even its sponsor is relieved to see it dead and officially buried.

— Robert Townsend

Bureaucracy is the epoxy that greases the wheels of progress.

— Jim Boren

If we did not have such a thing as an airplane today, we would probably create something the size of NASA to make one.

— H. Ross Perot

A committee can make a decision that is dumber than any of its members.

— David Coblitz

A committee is a cul-de-sac down which ideas are lured and then quietly strangled.

— Barnett Cocks

Any change is resisted because bureaucrats have a vested interest in the chaos in which they exist.

— Richard M. Nixon

The only thing that saves us from the bureaucracy is its inefficiency.
— Eugene McCarthy

Every revolution evaporates and leaves behind only the slime of a new bureaucracy.
Franz Kafka

A civil servant doesn't make jokes.
— Eugene Ionesco

A recent government publication on the marketing of cabbage contains, according to one report, 26,941 words. It is noteworthy in this regard that the Gettysburg Address contains a mere 279 words while the Lord's Prayer comprises but 67.
— Norman R. Augustine

Bureaucracy, the rule of no one, has become the modern form of despotism.
— Mary McCarthy

Too often I find that the volume of paper expands to fill the available briefcases.
— Jerry Brown

Bureaucrats write memoranda both because they appear to be busy when they are writing and because the memos, once written, immediately become proof that they were busy.
— Charles Peters

Bureaucracy defends the status quo long past the time when the quo has lost its status.
— Laurence J. Peter

If the copying machines that came along later had been here during the war, I'm not sure the Allies would have won. We'd all have drowned in paper.
— Alan Dickey

It seems to me that there must be an ecological limit to the number of paper pushers the earth can sustain, and that human civilization will collapse when the number of, say, tax lawyers exceeds the world's total population of farmers, weavers, fisherpersons, and pediatric nurses.
— Barbara Ehrenreich

The perfect bureaucrat everywhere is the man who manages to make no decisions and escape all responsibility.
— Brooks Atkinson

Meetings

To get something done, a committee should consist of no more than three men, two of whom are absent.

— *Robert Copeland*

A committee is a group that keeps minutes and loses hours.

— *Milton Berle*

Meetings are indispensable when you don't want to do anything.

—*John Kenneth Galbraith*

The optimum committee has no members.

— *Norman R. Augustine*

There is no monument dedicated to the memory of a committee.

— *Lester J. Pourciau*

If you see a snake, just kill it—don't appoint a committee on snakes.

— *H. Ross Perot*

A conference is a gathering of important people who singly can do nothing, but together can decide that nothing can be done.

— *Fred Allen*

$\mathcal{L}$eadership

The question "Who ought to be boss?" is like asking, "Who ought to be the tenor in the quartet?" Obviously, the man who can sing tenor. — *Henry Ford*

Good leaders make people feel that they're at the very heart of things, not at the periphery. Everyone feels that he or she makes a difference to the success of the organization. When that happens people feel centered and that gives their work meaning. — *Warren Bennis*

The great leaders are like the best conductors—they reach beyond the notes to reach the magic in the players. — *Blaine Lee*

I believe managing is like holding a dove in your hand. If you hold it too tightly you kill it, but if you hold it too loosely, you lose it. — *Tommy Lasorda*

The very essence of leadership is that you have to have vision. You can't blow an uncertain trumpet. — *Theodore Hesburgh*

The most important quality in a leader is that of being acknowledged as such. All leaders whose fitness is questioned are clearly lacking in force. — *André Maurois*

I am personally convinced that one person can be a change catalyst, a "transformer" in any situation, any organization. Such an individual is yeast that can leaven an entire loaf. It requires vision, initiative, patience, respect, persistence, courage, and faith to be a transforming leader. — *Stephen Covey*

I like my players to be married and in debt. That's the way you motivate them.
— *Ernie Banks*

Executives are like joggers. If you stop a jogger, he goes on running on the spot. If you drag an executive away from his business, he goes on running on the spot, pawing the ground, talking business. He never stops hurtling onwards, making decisions and executing them.
— *Jean Baudrillard*

I am certainly not one of those who need to be prodded. In fact, if anything, I am the prod.
— *Winston Churchill*

I am looking for a lot of men who have an infinite capacity to not know what can't be done.
— *Henry Ford*

The ultimate leader is one who is willing to develop people to the point that they eventually surpass him or her in knowledge and ability.
— *Fred A. Manske, Jr.*

Leadership is a combination of strategy and character. If you must be without one, be without the strategy.
— *H. Norman Schwarzkopf*

The leadership instinct you are born with is the backbone. You develop the funny bone and the wishbone that go with it.
— *Elaine Agather*

One of the tests of leadership is the ability to recognize a problem before it becomes an emergency.
— *Arnold Glasgow*

It is very hard to be a female leader. While it is assumed that any man, no matter how tough, has a soft side...a female leader is assumed to be one-dimensional.
— *Billie Jean King*

The first responsibility of a leader is to define reality. The last is to say thank you. In between, the leader is a servant.
— *Max De Pree*

I don't want any yes-men around me.
I want everybody to tell me the truth
even if it costs them their jobs.

— SAMUEL GOLDWYN

We still think of a powerful man as a born leader and a powerful woman as an anomaly.

— Margaret Atwood

Success in almost any field depends more on energy and drive than it does on intelligence. This explains why we have so many stupid leaders.

— Sloan Wilson

Motivation is everything. You can do the work of two people, but you can't be two people. Instead, you have to inspire the next guy down the line and get him to inspire his people.

— Lee Iacocca

Three billion people on the face of the earth go to bed hungry every night, but four billion people go to bed every night hungry for a simple word of encouragement and recognition.

— Cavett Robert

My grandfather once told me that there were two kinds of people: those who do the work and those who take the credit. He told me to try to be in the first group; there was much less competition.

— Indira Gandhi

No man will make a great leader who wants to do it all himself or get all the credit for doing it.

— Andrew Carnegie

The way to get things done is not to mind who gets the credit for doing them.

— Benjamin Jowett

Leadership is intangible, and therefore no weapon ever designed can replace it.

— Omar N. Bradley

Accept the fact that we have to treat almost anybody as a volunteer.   — *Peter F, Drucker*

Without initiative, leaders are simply workers in leadership positions.   — *Bo Bennett*

Fires can't be made with dead embers, nor can enthusiasm be stirred by spiritless men. Enthusiasm in our daily work lightens effort and turns even labor into pleasant tasks.
                                  — *James Baldwin*

Prosperity is a great teacher; adversity a greater.
                                  — *William Hazlitt*

Show me a poorly uniformed troop and I'll show you a poorly uniformed leader.   — *Robert Baden-Powell*

You get the best out of others when you give the best of yourself.   — *Harry Firestone*

The most important thing in communication is hearing what isn't said.   — *Peter F. Drucker*

The employer generally gets the employees he deserves.
                                  — *J. Paul Getty*

Example is not the main thing in influencing others. It is the only thing.   — *Albert Schweitzer*

Example has more followers than reason.
                                  — *Christian Nestell Bovee*

Eagles don't flock—you have to find them one at a time.
                                  — *H. Ross Perot*

If you pay peanuts, you get monkeys.
                                  — *James Goldsmith*

We're overpaying him, but he's worth it.

— *Samuel Goldwyn*

The view only changes for the lead dog.

— *Norman O. Brown*

If you want creative workers, give them enough time to play.

— *John Cleese*

In fact, I wanted to be John Cleese and it took some time to realize the job was in fact taken.　— *Douglas Adams*

The only risk of failure is promotion.

— *Scott Adams*

By working faithfully eight hours a day, you may get to be a boss and work twelve hours a day.　— *Robert Frost*

So much of what we call management consists in making it difficult for people to work.　— *Peter F. Drucker*

Make no little plans; they have no magic to stir men's blood and probably themselves will not be realized. Make big plans; aim high in hope and work, remembering that a noble, logical diagram once recorded will not die, but long after we are gone be a living thing, asserting itself with ever-growing insistence.　— *Daniel H. Burnham*

Don't tell people how to do things. Tell them what to do and let them surprise you with their results.　— *George S. Patton*

The question should be, Is it worth trying to do? not, Can it be done?　— *Allard Lowenstein*

No one has a greater asset for his business than a man's pride in his work.　— *Hosea Ballou*

Few things can help an individual more than to place responsibility on him, and to let him know that you trust him.
— *Booker T. Washington*

The people to fear are not those who disagree with you, but those who disagree with you and are too cowardly to let you know.
— *Napoleon Bonaparte*

A memorandum is written not to inform the reader but to protect the writer.
— *Dean Acheson*

Any task can be completed in only one-third more time than is currently estimated.
— *Norman R. Augustine*

Most projects start out slowly—and then sort of taper off.
— *Norman R. Augustine*

A small demerit extinguishes a long service.
— *Thomas Fuller*

A molehill man is a pseudo-busy executive who comes to work at 9 a.m. and finds a molehill on his desk. He has until 5 p.m. to make this molehill into a mountain. An accomplished molehill man will often have his mountain finished before lunch.
— *Fred Allen*

The longer the title, the less important the job.
— *George McGovern*

There is an enormous number of managers who have retired on the job.
— *Peter F. Drucker*

Habits are like supervisors that you don't notice.
— *Hannes Messemer*

There are two essential rules to management. One, the customer is always right; and two, they must be punished for their arrogance.
— *Scott Adams*

Media

A good newspaper, I suppose, is a nation talking to itself.
— *Arthur Miller*

When a dog bites a man, that is not news, because it happens so often. But if a man bites a dog, that is news.
— *John B. Bogart*

A newspaper is lumber made malleable. It is ink made into words and pictures. It is conceived, born, grows up and dies of old age in a day.
— *Jim Bishop*

Objective journalism and an opinion column are about as similar as the Bible and *Playboy* magazine.
— *Walter Cronkite*

Accuracy is to a newspaper what virtue is to a lady, but a newspaper can always print a retraction.
— *Adlai E. Stevenson*

With the newspaper strike on, I wouldn't consider dying.
— *Bette Davis*

I busted out of the place in a hurry and went to a saloon and drank beer and said that for the rest of my life I'd never take a job in a place where you couldn't throw cigarette butts on the floor. I was hooked on this writing for newspapers and magazines.
— *Jimmy Breslin*

I'm all in favor of keeping dangerous weapons out of the hands of fools. Let's start with typewriters.
— *Frank Lloyd Wright*

Rage is the only quality which has kept me, or anybody I have ever studied, writing columns for newspapers.
— *Jimmy Breslin*

We've uncovered some embarrassing ancestors in the not-too-distant past. Some horse thieves, and some people killed on Saturday nights. One of my relatives, unfortunately, was even in the newspaper business.   —Jimmy Carter

Never pick a fight with people who buy ink by the barrel.
      — Bill Clinton

Hot lead can be almost as effective coming from a linotype as from a firearm.   —John O'Hara

The pen is mightier than the sword, and considerably easier to write with.   — Marty Feldman

Four hostile newspapers are more to be feared than a thousand bayonets.   — Napoleon Bonaparte

It's amazing that the amount of news that happens in the world every day always just exactly fits the newspaper.
      —Jerry Seinfeld

What one has not experienced, one will never understand in print.   — Isadora Duncan

We tell the public which way the cat is jumping. The public will take care of the cat.   — Arthur Hays Sulzberger

A free press can, of course, be good or bad, but, most certainly without freedom, the press will never be anything but bad.
      — Albert Camus

Freedom of the press is limited to those who own one.
      — A. J. Liebling

You can never get all the facts from just one newspaper, and unless you have all the facts, you cannot make proper judgments about what is going on.   — Harry S. Truman

> During a recent panel on the numerous failures of American journalism, I proposed that almost all stories about government should begin: "Look out! They're about to smack you around again!"
>
> — MOLLY IVINS

Editor: a person employed by a newspaper, whose business it is to separate the wheat from the chaff, and to see that the chaff is printed.   *— Elbert Hubbard*

A journalist is a person who has mistaken his calling.
                                          — Otto von Bismarck

If one morning I walked on top of the water across the Potomac River, the headline that afternoon would read "President Can't Swim."   *— Lyndon B. Johnson*

I could announce one morning that the world was going to blow up in three hours and people would be calling in about my hair.   *— Katie Couric*

USA Today has come out with a new survey. Apparently, three out of every four people make up 75 percent of the population.   *— David Letterman*

Let blockheads read what blockheads wrote.
                                          — Warren Buffett

The dirtiest book of all is the expurgated book.
                                          — Walt Whitman

Journalism largely consists of saying "Lord Jones is dead" to people who never knew that Lord Jones was alive.
                                          — G. K. Chesterton

Trying to determine what is going on in the world by reading newspapers is like trying to tell the time by watching the second hand of a clock. — *Ben Hecht*

For most folks, no news is good news; for the press, good news is not news. — *Gloria Borger*

If I want to knock a story off the front page, I just change my hairstyle. — *Hillary Clinton*

It is part of prudence to thank an author for his book before reading it so as to avoid the necessity of lying about it afterwards. — *George Santayana*

Without words, without writing and without books there would be no history, there could be no concept of humanity. — *Hermann Hesse*

Do not read beauty magazines. They only make you feel ugly. — *Mary Schmich*

There's very little advice in men's magazines, because men don't think there's a lot they don't know. Women do. Women want to learn. Men think, "I know what I'm doing, just show me somebody naked." — *Jerry Seinfeld*

Before I refuse to take your questions, I have an opening statement. — *Ronald Reagan*

I'm just preparing my impromptu remarks. — *Winston Churchill*

Make sure you have finished speaking before your audience has finished listening. — *Dorothy Sarnoff*

Tell the audience what you're going to say, say it; then tell them what you've said. — *Dale Carnegie*

The public have an insatiable curiosity to know everything. Except what is worth knowing. Journalism, conscious of this, and having tradesman-like habits, supplies their demands.

— Oscar Wilde

What the mass media offers is not popular art, but entertainment which is intended to be consumed like food, forgotten, and replaced by a new dish. *— W. H. Auden*

The television, that insidious beast, that Medusa which freezes a billion people to stone every night, staring fixedly, that Siren which called and sang and promised so much and gave, after all, so little. *— Ray Bradbury*

The one function TV news performs very well is that when there is no news we give it to you with the same emphasis as if there were. *— David Brinkley*

Television news is like a lightning flash. It makes a loud noise, lights up everything around it, leaves everything else in darkness and then is suddenly gone. *— Hodding Carter*

When the politicians complain that TV turns the proceedings into a circus, it should be made clear that the circus was already there, and that TV has merely demonstrated that not all the performers are well trained. *— Edward R. Murrow*

And that's the way it is. *— Walter Cronkite*

Every time you think television has hit its lowest ebb, a new program comes along to make you wonder where you thought the ebb was. *— Art Buchwald*

If I turn on the television, am I to believe that that is America? I'm sorry, I don't believe that's America.

— Karen Black

When television came roaring in after the war they did a little school survey asking children which they preferred and why—television or radio. And there was this seven-year-old boy who said he preferred radio "because the pictures were better."

— *Alistair Cooke*

The new electronic independence re-creates the world in the image of a global village.

— *Marshall McLuhan*

Just because your voice reaches halfway around the world doesn't mean you are wiser than when it reached only to the end of the bar.

— *Edward R. Murrow*

I have learned that any fool can write a bad ad, but that it takes a real genius to keep his hands off a good one.

— *Leo Burnett*

Animation can explain whatever the mind of man can conceive. This facility makes it the most versatile and explicit means of communication yet devised for quick mass appreciation.

— *Walt Disney*

God cannot alter the past, though historians can.

— *Samuel Butler*

If we had three million exhibitionists and only one voyeur, nobody could make any money.

— *Albert Brooks*

Nobody believes the official spokesman . . . but everybody trusts an unidentified source.

— *Ron Nesen*

My advice to any diplomat who wants to have a good press is to have two or three kids and a dog.

— *Carl Rowan*

A reporter is always concerned with tomorrow. There's nothing tangible of yesterday. All I can say I've done is agitate the air 10 or 15 minutes and then boom—it's gone.

— *Edward R. Murrow*

I hate cameras. They are so much more sure than I am about everything.
John Steinbeck

A public-opinion poll is no substitute for thought.
— *Warren Buffett*

Those who cannot remember the past are condemned to repeat it.
— *George Santayana*

Never offend people with style when you can offend them with substance.
— *Sam Brown*

The function of the press in society is to inform, but its role in society is to make money.
— *A. J. Liebling*

Asking a working writer what he thinks about critics is like asking a lamppost how it feels about dogs.
— *Christopher Hampton*

A censor is a man who knows more than he thinks you ought to.
— *Granville Hicks*

Have you ever observed that we pay much more attention to a wise passage when it is quoted than when we read it in the original author?
— *Philip G. Hamerton*

When your work speaks for itself, don't interrupt.
— *Henry J. Kaiser*

The word *meaningful* when used today is nearly always meaningless.
— *Paul Johnson*

I take the view, and always have, that if you cannot say what you are going to say in 20 minutes you ought to go away and write a book about it.

— *Lord Brabazon*

News is history shot on the wing. The huntsmen from the Fourth Estate seek to bag only the peacock or the eagle of the swifting day. — *Gene Fowler*

I feel that if a person has problems communicating the very least he can do is to shut up. — *Tom Lehrer*

Drawing on my fine command of the English language, I said nothing. — *Robert Benchley*

Facts and truth really don't have much to do with each other. — *William Faulkner*

Every improvement in communication makes the bore more terrible. — *Frank Moore Colby*

Don't pay any attention to what they write about you. Just measure it in inches. — *Andy Warhol*

Fame

I don't think anyone should write their autobiography until after they're dead. — *Samuel Goldwyn*

Someday each of us will be famous for 15 minutes. — *Andy Warhol*

Now when I bore people at a party they think it's their fault. — *Henry Kissinger*

The celebrity is a person who is known for his well-knownness.
— *Daniel J. Boorstin*

If you have to have a job in this world, a high-priced movie star is a pretty good gig.
— *Tom Hanks*

When Ginger Rogers danced with Astaire, it was the only time in the movies when you looked at the man, not the woman.
— *Gene Kelly*

Everyone wants to be Cary Grant. Even I want to be Cary Grant.
— *Cary Grant*

Nobody can be exactly like me. Even I have trouble doing it.
— *Tallulah Bankhead*

Glamour is what I sell. It's my stock in trade.
— *Marlene Dietrich*

A celebrity has just as much right to speak out as people who hold real jobs. This is America, after all, and you should not be precluded from voicing your opinions just because you sing songs, mouth other people's words on a sitcom or, for that matter, spin a giant multicolored wheel on a game show.
— *Pat Sajak*

If anyone asks you what kind of music you play, tell him "pop." Don't tell him "rock 'n' roll" or they won't even let you in the hotel.
— *Buddy Holly*

One thing about being successful is that I stopped being afraid of dying. Once you're a star you're dead already. You're embalmed.
— *Dustin Hoffman*

An actor's a guy who, if you ain't talking about him, ain't listening.
— *Marlon Brando*

You know, when I first went into the movies Lionel Barrymore played my grandfather. Later he played my father and finally he played my husband. If he had lived I'm sure I would have played his mother. That's the way it is in Hollywood. The men get younger and the women get older. *— Lillian Gish*

The only reason I'm in Hollywood is that I don't have the moral courage to refuse the money. *— Marlon Brando*

I'm Chevy Chase and you're not. *— Chevy Chase*

Life is like a B-picture script! It is that corny. If I had my life story offered to me to film, I'd turn it down. *— Kirk Douglas*

I have been very happy, very rich, very beautiful, much adulated, very famous and very unhappy. *— Brigitte Bardot*

You're not a star until they can spell your name in Karachi. *— Humphrey Bogart*

Give me a couple of years, and I'll make that actress an overnight success. *— Samuel Goldwyn*

Don't get me wrong, I'm very thankful for all the aliens I've met and loved. *—Jonathan Frakes*

I am a commentator, not a brain surgeon. I do not save people's lives. Knowing that I am not more important than anyone else, that I go on the air at 9 o'clock and then off again at 10 really puts things in perspective. This kind of awareness is important to anyone who has risen to prominence in their chosen career, for falling down can be much harder than rising up. *— Larry King*

A celebrity is a person who works hard all his life to become well known, then wears dark glasses to avoid being recognized. *— Fred Allen*

Its better to be known by six people for something you're proud of than by 60 million for something you're not.

— *Albert Brooks*

Actors have bodyguards and entourages not because anybody wants to hurt them—who would want to hurt an actor?—but because they want to get recognized. God forbid someone doesn't recognize them.

— *James Caan*

If you want a place in the sun, you've got to expect a few blisters.

— *Abigail Van Buren*

Fame is a fickle food upon a shifting plate. *Justia*

— *Emily Dickinson*

I'm never going to be famous. I don't do anything, not one single thing. I used to bite my nails, but I don't even do that anymore.

— *Dorothy Parker*

Even though people may be well known, they hold in their hearts the emotions of a simple person for the moments that are the most important of those we know on earth: birth, marriage and death.

— *Jackie Kennedy Onassis*

I had pro offers from the Detroit Lions and Green Bay Packers, who were pretty hard up for linemen in those days. If I had gone into professional football the name Jerry Ford might have been a household word today.

— *Gerald R. Ford*

It wasn't until the Nobel Prize that they really thawed out. They couldn't understand my books, but they could understand $30,000.

— *William Faulkner*

My mother was against me being an actress—until I introduced her to Frank Sinatra.

— ANGIE DICKINSON

To be great is to be misunderstood.

— Ralph Waldo Emerson

Fame—a few words upon a tombstone, and the truth of those not to be depended on. *— Christian Nestell Bovee*

A celebrity is one who is known to many persons he is glad he doesn't know. *— H. L. Mencken*

A sign of celebrity is that his name is often worth more than his services. *— Daniel J. Boorstin*

Standing ovations have become far too commonplace. What we need are ovations where the audience members all punch and kick one another. *— George Carlin*

I get a standing ovation just standing.

— George Burns

It took me fifteen years to discover that I had no talent for writing, but I couldn't give it up because by that time I was too famous. *— Robert Benchley*

A celebrity is anyone who looks like he spends more than two hours working on his hair. *— Steve Martin*

Fame is only good for one thing—they will cash your check in a small town. *— Truman Capote*

Hollywood is a place where people from Iowa mistake each other for stars. *— Fred Allen*

Hollywood is a place where a man can get stabbed in the back while climbing a ladder. *— William Faulkner*

Fame is like a shaved pig with a greased tail, and it is only after it has slipped through the hands of some thousands, that some fellow, by mere chance, holds on to it! *— Davy Crockett*

I regret the passing of the studio system. I was very appreciative of it because I had no talent   *— Lucille Ball*

Celebrity was a long time in coming; it will go away. Everything goes away.   *— Carol Burnett*

I don't deserve this award, but I have arthritis and I don't deserve that either.   *—Jack Benny*

Fame usually comes to those who are thinking about something else.   *— Oliver Wendell Holmes*

$\mathscr{T}$echnology

Men have become the tools of their tools.
                    — Henry David Thoreau

Our Age of Anxiety is, in great part, the result of trying to do today's jobs with yesterday's tools.   *— Marshall McLuhan*

Humanity is acquiring all the right technology for all the wrong reasons.   *— R. Buckminster Fuller*

Is fuel efficiency really what we need most desperately? I say that what we really need is a car that can be shot when it breaks down.
                    — Russell Baker

The best car safety device is a rearview mirror with a cop in it.
                    — Dudley Moore

People can have the Model T in any color—so long as it's
black.   *— Henry Ford*

I know a lot about cars. I can look at a car's headlights and
tell you exactly which way it's coming.   *— Mitch Hedberg*

To invent, you need a good imagination and a pile of junk.
                                              — Thomas Alva Edison

A specification that will not fit on one page of 8.5 x 11-inch
paper cannot be understood.   *— Mark Ardis*

Inanimate objects can be classified scientifically into three
major categories; those that don't work, those that break
down and those that get lost.   *— Russell Baker*

The shortest distance between two points is under construction.
                                                 — Noelie Altito

It is no coincidence that in no known language does the
phrase "as pretty as an airport" appear.   *— Douglas Adams*

Our scientific power has outrun our spiritual power. We have
guided missiles and misguided men.
                                            — Martin Luther King, Jr.

The first rule of any technology used in a business is that
automation applied to an efficient operation will magnify
the efficiency. The second is that automation applied to an
inefficient operation will magnify the inefficiency. *— Bill Gates*

Bill Gates is a very rich man today...and do you want to
know why? The answer is one word: versions.   *— Dave Barry*

At the present rate of progress, it is almost impossible to
imagine any technical feat that cannot be achieved—if it can
be achieved at all—within the next few hundred years.
                                              — Arthur C. Clarke

The robot is going to lose. Not by much. But when the final score is tallied, flesh and blood is going to beat the damn monster.
— *Adam Smith*

I do not fear computers. I fear lack of them.
— *Isaac Asimov*

The most likely way for the world to be destroyed, most experts agree, is by accident. That's where we come in; we're computer professionals. We cause accidents.
— *Nathaniel Borenstein*

To err is human—and to blame it on a computer is even more so.
— *Robert Orben*

If it keeps up, man will atrophy all his limbs but the push-button finger.
— FRANK LLOYD WRIGHT

The future is here. It's just not widely distributed yet.
— *William Gibson*

I want to put a ding in the universe.
— *Steve Jobs*

Never trust a computer you can't throw out a window.
— *Steve Wozniak*

I think computer viruses should count as life. I think it says something about human nature that the only form of life we have created so far is purely destructive. We've created life in our own image.
— *Stephen Hawking*

The first rule of intelligent tinkering is to save all the parts.
— *Paul Ehrlich*

Oh, I never look under the hood.
— *E. B. White*

Programming is like sex: one mistake and you have to support it for the rest of your life. — *Michael Sinz*

The danger from computers is not that they will eventually get as smart as men, but we will meanwhile agree to meet them halfway. — *Bernard Avishai*

To err is human, but to really foul things up you need a computer. — *Paul Ehrlich*

The great thing about a computer notebook is that no matter how much you stuff into it, it doesn't get bigger or heavier. — *Bill Gates*

A computer lets you make more mistakes faster than any invention in human history—with the possible exceptions of handguns and tequila. — *Mitch Ratliffe*

My favorite thing about the Internet is that you get to go into the private world of real creeps without having to smell them. — *Penn Jillette*

I used to think that cyberspace was 50 years away. What I thought was 50 years away, was only 10 years away. And what I thought was 10 years away...it was already here. I just wasn't aware of it yet. — *Bruce Sterling*

The real problem is not whether machines think but whether men do. — *B. F. Skinner*

Programming today is a race between software engineers striving to build bigger and better idiot-proof programs, and the Universe trying to produce bigger and better idiots. So far, the Universe is winning. — *Rich Cook*

In all large corporations, there is a pervasive fear that someone, somewhere is having fun with a computer on company time. Networks help alleviate that fear. — *John C. Dvorak*

We've heard that a million monkeys at a million keyboards could produce the complete works of Shakespeare. Now, thanks to the Internet, we know that is not true. — *Robert Wilensky*

Looking at the proliferation of personal Web pages on the Net, it looks like very soon everyone on earth will have 15 megabytes of fame. — *M. G. Siriam*

Ours is the age that is proud of machines that think and suspicious of men who try to. — *H. Mumford Jones*

It can take quite a while for a Web page to appear on your screen. The reason for the delay is that, when you type in a Web address, your computer passes it along to another computer, which in turn passes it along to another computer, and so on through as many as five computers before it finally reaches the work station of a disgruntled U.S. Postal Service employee, who throws it in the trash. — *Dave Barry*

A common mistake that people make when trying to design something completely foolproof is to underestimate the ingenuity of complete fools. — *Douglas Adams*

Never worry about theory as long as the machinery does what it's supposed to do. — *Robert A. Heinlein*

Technology is the knack of so arranging the world that we don't have to experience it. — *Max Frisch*

I have always hated machinery, and the only machine I ever understood was a wheel-barrow, and that but imperfectly. — *E. T. Bell*

The nice thing about standards is that there are so many of them to choose from. — *Andrew S. Tanenbaum*

The days of the digital watch are numbered. — *Tom Stoppard*

Aircraft flight in the 21st century will always be in a westerly direction, preferably supersonic, crossing time zones to provide the additional hours needed to fix the broken electronics.

— *Norman R. Augustine*

If we had a reliable way to label our toys good and bad, it would be easy to regulate technology wisely. But we can rarely see far enough ahead to know which road leads to damnation.

— *Freeman Dyson*

People are broad-minded. They'll accept the fact that a person can be an alcoholic, a dope fiend, a wife beater and even a newspaperman, but if a man doesn't drive, there's something wrong with him.

— *Art Buchwald*

The best way to predict the future is to invent it.

— *Alan Kay*

In the information age, you don't teach philosophy as they did after feudalism. You perform it. If Aristotle were alive today he'd have a talk show.

— *Timothy Leary*

For a successful technology, reality must take precedence over public relations, for Nature cannot be fooled.

— *Richard Feynman*

One machine can do the work of 50 ordinary men. No machine can do the work of one extraordinary man.

— *Elbert Hubbard*

We are more ready to try the untried when what we do is inconsequential. Hence the fact that many inventions had their birth as toys.

— *Eric Hoffer*

Engineers like to solve problems. If there are no problems handily available, they will create their own problems.

— *Scott Adams*

Stress

A woman is like a tea bag—you never know how strong she is until she gets in hot water. — *Eleanor Roosevelt*

Accomplishing the impossible means only that the boss will add it to your regular duties. — *Doug Larson*

I don't know the key to success, but the key to failure is trying to please everybody. — *Bill Cosby*

Plan your work, work your plan. Lack of system produces that "I'm swamped" feeling. — *Norman Vincent Peale*

There cannot be a crisis next week. My schedule is already full. — *Henry Kissinger*

There is a vast world of work out there in this country, where at least 111 million people are employed in this country alone—many of whom are bored out of their minds. All day long. Not for nothing is their motto TGIF—"Thank God It's Friday." They live for the weekends, when they can go do what they really want to do.
— *Richard Nelson Bolles*

All paid jobs absorb and degrade the mind. — *Aristotle*

Half the battle in alleviating stress involves knowing how to handle new information that crosses your desk.
— *Jeff Davidson*

Anyone who says he won't resign four times, will.
— *John Kenneth Galbraith*

The way to get five weeks of vacation is to have open-heart surgery. It is the perfect cover. Bipolar depression is a downer and TB makes your friends nervous and a hip replacement is terribly inconvenient, but cardiac surgery poses few risks, is mostly painless, and has a grandeur about it that erases all obligations, social and professional. It is the Get Out of Work card.

— *Garrison Keillor*

Everyone rises to their level of incompetence.

— *Laurence J. Peter*

Getting fired is nature's way of telling you that you had the wrong job in the first place.

— *Hal Lancaster*

No man ever listened himself out of a job.

— *Calvin Coolidge*

If you want to gather honey, don't kick over the beehive.

— *Dale Carnegie*

If you aren't fired with enthusiasm, you will be fired with enthusiasm.

— *Vince Lombardi*

Gain a modest reputation for being unreliable and you will never be asked to do a thing.

— *Paul Theroux*

One of the symptoms of an approaching nervous breakdown is the belief that one's work is terribly important.

— *Bertrand Russell*

It is difficult to get a man to understand something when his job depends on not understanding it.

— *Upton Sinclair*

You don't get anything clean without getting something else dirty.

— *Cecil Baxter*

My second favorite household chore is ironing. My first being hitting my head on the top bunk bed until I faint.

— *Erma Bombeck*

MODERN LIFE

> A psychiatrist is a fellow who asks you
> a lot of expensive questions your wife
> asks for nothing.
>
> — JOEY ADAMS

You make the beds, you wash the dishes, and six months later
you have to start all over again. — *Joan Rivers*

What the world really needs is more love and less paperwork.
— *Pearl Bailey*

Open your mail over the wastebasket. — *Jeff Davidson*

You moon the wrong person at an office party and suddenly
you're not "professional" anymore. — *Jeff Foxworthy*

Informed decision-making comes from a long tradition of
guessing and then blaming others for inadequate results.
— *Scott Adams*

Advice is like castor oil, easy enough to give but dreadful
uneasy to take. — *Josh Billings*

The price one pays for pursuing any profession or calling is
an intimate knowledge of its ugly side. — *James Baldwin*

Turbulence is life force. It is opportunity. Let's love turbulence and use it for change. — *Ramsey Clark*

Habit is the denial of creativity and the negation of freedom;
a self-imposed straitjacket of which the wearer is unaware.
— *Arthur Koestler*

Are we having fun yet? — *Carol Burnett*

The human brain starts working the moment you are born
and never stops until you stand up to speak in public.
— *George Jessel*

An objection is not a rejection; it is simply a request for more information.
— *Bo Bennett*

America is the country where you buy a lifetime supply of aspirin for one dollar and use it up in two weeks.
—*John Barrymore*

When you are not physically starving, you have the luxury to realize psychic and emotional starvation.
— *Cherrie Moraga*

When Solomon said there was a time and a place for everything he had not encountered the problem of parking his automobile.
— *Bob Edwards*

Believe, when you are most unhappy, that there is something for you to do in the world. So long as you can sweeten another's pain, life is not in vain.
— *Helen Keller*

The most difficult thing in the world is to know how to do a thing and to watch someone else do it wrong, without comment.
— *T. H. White*

Each man is afraid of his neighbor's disapproval—a thing which, to the general run of the human race, is more dreaded than wolves and death.
— *Mark Twain*

If you're going through hell, keep going.
— *Walt Disney*

I believe in trusting. Trust begets trust. Suspicion is fetid and only stinks. He who trusts has never yet lost in the world.
— *Mahatma Gandhi*

Have you ever noticed? Anybody going slower than you is an idiot, and anyone going faster than you is a moron.
— *George Carlin*

Three o'clock is always too late or too early for anything you want to do.
—*Jean-Paul Sartre*

MODERN LIFE

If we were all given by magic the power to read each other's thoughts, I suppose the first effect would be to dissolve all friendships. — *Bertrand Russell*

Happiness is having a large, loving, caring, close-knit family in another city. — *George Burns*

Man does not live by words alone, despite the fact that sometimes he has to eat them. — *Adlai E. Stevenson*

tyle

Fashion can be bought.
Style one must possess. — *Edna Woolman Chase*

I base my fashion taste on what doesn't itch. — *Gilda Radner*

Where lipstick is concerned, the important thing is not color, but to accept God's final word on where your lips end. — *Jerry Seinfeld*

I can't take a well-tanned person seriously. — *Cleveland Amory*

She got her looks from her father. He's a plastic surgeon. — *Groucho Marx*

Every generation laughs at the old fashions but religiously follows the new. — *Henry David Thoreau*

Comedians Gone Wise

Offstage, comedians pay bills, tie their shoes, and hunt for parking spaces just like the rest of us. They're good at what they do because they're keen observers of humankind and because they're good communicators. Here are some of their serious thoughts—more wise than wisecracking.

Laughter is the closest distance between two people.

— Victor Borge

A bookstore is one of the only pieces of evidence we have that people are still thinking.

— Jerry Seinfeld

Talent alone won't make you a success. Neither will being in the right place at the right time, unless you are ready. The most important question is: "Are you ready?"

— Johnny Carson

Look, I don't want to wax philosophic, but I will say that if you're alive you've got to flap your arms and legs, you've got to jump around a lot, for life is the very opposite of death, and therefore you must at very least think noisy and colorfully, or you're not alive.

— Mel Brooks

If you want something done, ask a busy person to do it. The more things you do, the more you can do.

— Lucille Ball

You're only given a little spark of madness. You mustn't lose it.

— Robin Williams

The heart of marriage is memories; and if the two of you happen to have the same ones and can savor your reruns, then your marriage is a gift from the gods. — Bill Cosby

If you have it and you know you have it, then you have it. If you have it and don't know you have it, you don't have it. If you don't have it but you think you have it, then you have it.

— Jackie Gleason

I've had a few arguments with people, but I never carry a grudge. You know why? While you're carrying a grudge, they're out dancing.

— Buddy Hackett

Throughout life people will make you mad, disrespect you and treat you bad. Let God deal with the things they do, 'cause hate in your heart will consume you too. — Will Smith

Failure seldom stops you. What stops you is the fear of failure.

— Jack Lemmon

The greatest thing you can do is surprise yourself.

— Steve Martin

Laughter gives us distance. It allows us to step back from an event, deal with it and then move on. — Bob Newhart

Armageddon is not around the corner. This is only what the people of violence want us to believe. The complexity and diversity of the world is the hope for the future. — Michael Palin

If you send out good people into the world, you know you've done something good. — Carl Reiner

Live by this credo: Have a little laugh at life and look around you for happiness instead of sadness. Laughter has always brought me out of unhappy situations. — Red Skelton

These are my new shoes. They're good shoes.
They won't make you rich like me,
they won't make you rebound like me,
they definitely won't make you handsome
like me. They'll only make you have shoes
like me. That's it.

— CHARLES BARKLEY

I've exercised with women so thin that buzzards followed
them to their cars.
— *Erma Bombeck*

Luxury must be comfortable, otherwise it is not luxury.
— *Coco Chanel*

If you stay in Beverly Hills too long you become a Mercedes.
— *Robert Redford*

I will buy any creme, cosmetic, or elixir from a woman with
a European accent.
— *Erma Bombeck*

She was what we used to call a suicide blond—dyed by her
own hand.
— *Saul Bellow*

Fashion is what you adopt when you don't know who you are.
— *Quentin Crisp*

I think that the most important thing a woman can have—
next to talent, of course—is her hairdresser.
— *Joan Crawford*

Darling, the legs aren't so beautiful. I just know what to do
with them.
— *Marlene Dietrich*

Plain women know more about men than beautiful women do.
— *Katharine Hepburn*

I always say shopping is cheaper than a psychiatrist.
— *Tammy Faye Bakker*

I buy expensive suits. They just look cheap on me.

— *Warren Buffett*

It is amazing how complete is the delusion that beauty is goodness. — *Leo Tolstoy*

Put even the plainest woman into a beautiful dress and unconsciously she will try to live up to it.

— *Lucie Duff-Gordon*

Beauty is mysterious as well as terrible. God and devil are fighting there, and the battlefield is the heart of man.

— *Fyodor Dostoyevsky*

I always say that beauty is only sin deep. — *Saki (Hector Hugh Monro)*

A thing of beauty is a joy forever. —*John Keats*

I never go out unless I look like Joan Crawford the movie star. If you want to see the girl next door, go next door.

—*Joan Crawford*

Women are most fascinating between the ages of 35 and 40 after they have won a few races and know how to pace themselves. Since few women ever pass 40, maximum fascination can continue indefinitely. — *Christian Dior*

My religious background is that my mother is a Christian Dior Scientist. — *Robin Williams*

A man of 80 has outlived probably three new schools of painting, two of architecture and poetry and a hundred in dress. — *Lord Byron*

Art produces ugly things which frequently become more beautiful with time. Fashion, on the other hand, produces beautiful things which always become ugly with time.

—*Jean Cocteau*

Fallacies do not cease to be fallacies because they become fashions.
— *G. K. Chesterton*

Women thrive on novelty and are easy meat for the commerce of fashion. Men prefer old pipes and torn jackets.
— *Anthony Burgess*

It is easy to be beautiful; it is difficult to appear so.
— *Hosea Ballou*

I think I'm vaguely blonde. To be perfectly frank, I don't know.
— *Cate Blanchett*

Going hungry never bothered me—it was having no clothes.
— *Cher*

No matter what a woman looks like, if she's confident, she's sexy.
— *Paris Hilton*

The fashion wears out more apparel than the man.
— *William Shakespeare*

If men can run the world, why can't they stop wearing neckties? How intelligent is it to start the day by tying a little noose around your neck?
— *Linda Ellerbee*

We seem to believe it is possible to ward off death by following rules of good grooming.
— *Don DeLillo*

In Cleveland there is legislation moving forward to ban people from wearing pants that fit too low. However, there is lots of opposition from the plumbers union.
— *Conan O'Brien*

A little bad taste is like a nice dash of paprika.
— *Dorothy Parker*

 Money

The trouble with the rat race is that even if you win, you're still a rat.
— *Lily Tomlin*

The only thing money gives you is the freedom of not worrying about money.
— *Johnny Carson*

Whoever said money can't buy happiness simply didn't know where to go shopping.
— *Bo Derek*

Retirement at sixty-five is ridiculous. When I was sixty-five I still had pimples.
— *George Burns*

Admit it, sport-utility-vehicle owners! It's shaped a little differently, but it's a station wagon! And you do not drive it across rivers! You drive it across the Wal-Mart parking lot!
— *Dave Barry*

Don't simply retire from something; have something to retire to.
— *Harry Emerson Fosdick*

A lawyer starts life giving $500 worth of law for $5 and ends giving $5 worth for $500.
— *Benjamin H. Brewster*

Normal is getting dressed in clothes that you buy for work, driving through traffic in a car that you are still paying for, in order to get to a job that you need so you can pay for the clothes, car and the house that you leave empty all day in order to afford to live in it.
— *Ellen Goodman*

It's diamonds in your pockets one week, macaroni and cheese the next.
— *Jolene Blalock*

If it isn't the sheriff, it's the finance company; I've got more attachments on me than a vacuum cleaner.   — *John Barrymore*

Although most products will soon be too costly to purchase, there will be a thriving market in the sale of books on how to fix them.   — *Norman R. Augustine*

Inflation is bringing us true democracy. For the first time in history, luxuries and necessities are selling at the same price.
                                   — *Robert Orben*

Why grab possessions like thieves, or divide them like social-ists when you can ignore them like wise men?
                                   — *Natalie Clifford Barney*

I bought some batteries, but they weren't included.
                                   — *Steven Wright*

In spite of the cost of living, it's still popular.
                                   — *Laurence J. Peter*

There are plenty of good five-cent cigars in the country. The trouble is they cost a quarter. What this country needs is a good five-cent nickel.   — *Franklin P. Adams*

Why is there so much month left at the end of the money?
                                   — *John Barrymore*

No one goes there nowadays. It's too crowded.
                                   — *Yogi Berra*

I'm spending a year dead for tax reasons.
                                   — *Douglas Adams*

Big business never pays a nickel in taxes, according to Ralph Nader, who represents a big consumer organization that never pays a nickel in taxes.   — *Dave Barry*

The hardest thing in the world to understand is income tax.
— *Albert Einstein*

The income tax has made more liars out of the American people than golf has.
— *Will Rogers*

Every crowd has a silver lining.
— *P. T. Barnum*

People will buy anything that is one to a customer.
— *Sinclair Lewis*

Take all the fools out of this world and there wouldn't be any fun living in it, or profit.
— *Josh Billings*

There is only one boss: the customer. And he can fire everybody in the company, from the chairman on down, simply by spending his money somewhere else.
— *Sam Walton*

Your most unhappy customers are your greatest source of learning.
— *Bill Gates*

The safest way to double your money is to fold it over and put it in your pocket.
— *Kin Hubbard*

Money is the most egalitarian force in society. It confers power on whoever holds it.
— *Roger Starr*

People who work sitting down get paid more than people who work standing up.
— *Ogden Nash*

All work and no play makes Jack a dull boy—and Jill a wealthy widow.
— *Evan Esar*

Every time you spend money, you're casting a vote for the kind of world you want.

— ANNA LAPPE

The only really good place to buy lumber is at a store where the lumber has already been cut and attached together in the form of furniture, finished, and put inside boxes.

— *Dave Barry*

Why pay a dollar for a bookmark? Why not use the dollar for a bookmark?
— *Steven Spielberg*

If we could sell our experiences for what they cost us, we'd all be millionaires.
— *Abigail Van Buren*

Free advice is worth the price.
— *Robert Half*

If your imagination leads you to understand how quickly people grant your requests when those requests appeal to their self-interest, you can have practically anything you go after.
— *Napoleon Hill*

Advertising may be described as the science of arresting human intelligence long enough to get money from it.
— *Stephen Leacock*

What is the difference between unethical and ethical advertising? Unethical advertising uses falsehoods to deceive the public; ethical advertising uses truth to deceive the public.
— *Vilhjalmur Stefansson*

A great ad campaign will make a bad product fail faster. It will get more people to know it's bad.
— *William Bernbach*

Half the money I spend on advertising is wasted; the trouble is I don't know which half.
—*John Wanamaker*

Few people at the beginning of the nineteenth century needed an adman to tell them what they wanted.
—*John Kenneth Galbraith*

We grew up founding our dreams on the infinite promise of American advertising. I still believe that one can learn to play the piano by mail and that mud will give you a perfect complexion.

— *Zelda Fitzgerald*

Advertising is a valuable economic factor because it is the cheapest way of selling goods, particularly if the goods are worthless.

— *Sinclair Lewis*

The philosophy behind much advertising is based on the old observation that every man is really two men—the man he is and the man he wants to be.

— *William Feather*

Too many of us look upon Americans as dollar chasers. This is a cruel libel, even if it is reiterated thoughtlessly by the Americans themselves.

— *Albert Einstein*

He who will not economize will have to agonize.

— *Confucius*

Finance is the art of passing currency from hand to hand until it finally disappears.

— *Robert W. Sarnoff*

Money, it turned out, was exactly like sex. You thought of nothing else if you didn't have it and thought of other things if you did.

— *James Baldwin*

Money is a singular thing. It ranks with love as man's greatest source of joy. And with death as his greatest source of anxiety. Over all history it has oppressed nearly all people in one of two ways: either it has been abundant and very unreliable, or reliable and very scarce.

— *John Kenneth Galbraith*

Advertising is the modern substitute for argument; its function is to make the worse appear the better.

— *George Santayana*

A bank is a place where they lend you an umbrella in fair weather and ask for it back when it begins to rain.

— *Robert Frost*

I hate banks. They do nothing positive for anybody except take care of themselves. They're first in with their fees and first out when there's trouble.

— *Earl Warren*

If you owe the bank $100, that's your problem. If you owe the bank $100 million, that's the bank's problem.

—*J. Paul Getty*

A bank is a place that will lend you money if you can prove that you don't need it.

— *Bob Hope*

Never invest in a business you cannot understand.

—WARREN BUFFETT

Banking establishments are more dangerous than standing armies.

— *Thomas Jefferson*

Drive-in banks were established so most of the cars today could see their real owners.

— *E. Joseph Crossman*

An economist is a man who states the obvious in terms of the incomprehensible.

— *Alfred A. Knopf*

I guess I should warn you, if I turn out to be particularly clear, you've probably misunderstood what I've said.

— *Alan Greenspan*

An economist is an expert who will know tomorrow why the things he predicted yesterday didn't happen today.

— *Laurence J. Peter*

MODERN LIFE

A study of economics usually reveals that the best time to buy anything is last year
— Marty Allen

If all economists were laid end to end, they would not reach a conclusion.
— George Bernard Shaw

Economics is extremely useful as a form of employment for economists.
—John Kenneth Galbraith

Risk comes from not knowing what you're doing.
— Warren Buffett

If stock market experts were so expert, they would be buying stock, not selling advice.
— Norman R. Augustine

A speculator is a man who observes the future, and acts before it occurs.
— Bernard Baruch

Emotions are your worst enemy in the stock market.
— Don Hays

Don't try to buy at the bottom and sell at the top. It can't be done except by liars.
— Bernard Baruch

The business of America is business.
— Calvin Coolidge

You can close more business in two months by becoming interested in other people than you can in two years by trying to get people interested in you.
— Dale Carnegie

Small opportunities are often the beginning of great enterprises.
— Demosthenes

I have probably purchased 50 "hot tips" in my career, maybe even more. When I put them all together, I know I am a net loser.
— Charles Schwab

That which costs little is less valued.
— Miguel de Cervantes

People want economy and they will pay any price to get it.

— Lee Iacocca

A billion saved is a billion earned.

— Norman R. Augustine

The only reason I made a commercial for American Express was to pay for my American Express bill.   *— Peter Ustinov*

I don't think meals have any business being deductible. I'm for separation of calories and corporations.   *— Ralph Nader*

If past history was all there was to the game, the richest people would be librarians.   *— Warren Buffett*

Always listen to experts. They'll tell you what can't be done and why. Then do it.   *— Robert A. Heinlein*

An expert is a person who has made all the mistakes that can be made in a very narrow field.   *— Niels Bohr*

Much ingenuity with a little money is vastly more profitable and amusing than much money without ingenuity.

— Arnold Bennett

Anyone who says businessmen deal in facts, not fiction, has never read old five-year projections.   *— Malcolm Forbes*

The best minds are not in government. If any were, business would steal them away.   *— Ronald Reagan*

Oil prices have fallen lately. We include this news for the benefit of gas stations, which otherwise wouldn't learn of it for six months.

— BILL TAMMEUS

MODERN LIFE

There are many highly successful businesses in the United States. There are also many highly paid executives. The policy is not to intermingle the two. — *Norman R. Augustine*

Capital isn't so important in business. Experience isn't so important. You can get both these things. What is important is ideas. If you have ideas, you have the main asset you need, and there isn't any limit to what you can do with your business and your life. — *Harvey S. Firestone*

Capitalism needs to function like a game of tug-of-war. Two opposing sides need to continually struggle for dominance, but at no time can either side be permitted to walk away with the rope. — *Pete Holiday*

I don't want to do business with those who don't make a profit, because they can't give the best service.
— *Richard Bach*

Every economy is uncertain. Referring to this or any economy as "uncertain" is an unnecessary and pessimistic redundancy.
— *Bo Bennett*

Business, that's easily defined—it's other people's money.
— *Peter F. Drucker*

If you work just for money, you'll never make it, but if you love what you're doing and you always put the customer first, success will be yours. — *Ray Kroc*

Corporation: An ingenious device for obtaining profit without individual responsibility. — *Ambrose Bierce*

The use of solar energy has not been opened up because the oil industry does not own the sun. — *Ralph Nader*

Business opportunities are like buses, there's always another one coming. — *Richard Branson*

ℐndex

A Gift For

_____

Presented By

_____

_____